T0319033

Cambridge Elements ≡

Elements in the Economics of Emerging Markets
edited by
Bruno S. Sergi
Harvard University

THE ECONOMICS OF DIGITAL SHOPPING IN CENTRAL AND EASTERN EUROPE

Barbara Grabiwoda
Publicis Commerce

Bogdan Mróz
SGH Warsaw School of Economics

CAMBRIDGE
UNIVERSITY PRESS

CAMBRIDGE
UNIVERSITY PRESS

University Printing House, Cambridge CB2 8BS, United Kingdom

One Liberty Plaza, 20th Floor, New York, NY 10006, USA

477 Williamstown Road, Port Melbourne, VIC 3207, Australia

314–321, 3rd Floor, Plot 3, Splendor Forum, Jasola District Centre,
New Delhi – 110025, India

103 Penang Road, #05–06/07, Visioncrest Commercial, Singapore 238467

Cambridge University Press is part of the University of Cambridge.

It furthers the University's mission by disseminating knowledge in the pursuit of
education, learning, and research at the highest international levels of excellence.

www.cambridge.org
Information on this title: www.cambridge.org/9781009108447
DOI: 10.1017/9781009104302

© Barbara Grabiwoda and Bogdan Mróz 2022

First published 2022

A catalogue record for this publication is available from the British Library.

ISBN 978-1-009-10844-7 Paperback
ISSN 2631-8598 (online)
ISSN 2631-858X (print)

The Economics of Digital Shopping in Central and Eastern Europe

Elements in the Economics of Emerging Markets

DOI: 10.1017/9781009104302
First published online: February 2022

Barbara Grabiwoda
Publicis Commerce

Bogdan Mróz
SGH Warsaw School of Economics

Author for correspondence: Bogdan Mróz, bogdan.mroz@sgh.waw.pl

Abstract: Transformations caused by increasing virtual connectivity reach all business touchpoints, but the surge towards digital technologies is not distributed evenly across European markets, with the Central and Eastern Europe (CEE) region showing the strongest diversity of digital adoption levels. This Element outlines the characteristics of CEE digital markets, along with an additional contextual layer investigating online consumer behaviors. In-depth analysis of the similarities and differences in the region will allow the pace of ongoing digitization to be traced. The authors' objective in delivering this Element is to analyze the opportunities presented by the digital economy in CEE and to provide an actionable outlook for the e-commerce potential within the region's markets. Observations are based on in-depth analysis of dependencies between globalization of consumer behaviors and ongoing barriers to digital adoption caused by both economic and geo-political limitations.

Keywords: digital shopping, e-commerce, Central and Eastern Europe, digital transformation, COVID-19 pandemic

ISBNs: 9781009108447 (PB), 9781009104302 (OC)
ISSNs: 2631-8598 (online), 2631-858X (print)

Contents

Introduction

The evolution of digital technology is one of the most significant drivers of change in consumer behavior in the twenty-first century. Markets and businesses are constantly challenged by how important digital connectivity is becoming to consumers.

Western Europe is still the most developed e-commerce market in Europe, accounting for 70 percent of the total e-commerce value on the continent and the highest share of online shoppers (83 percent) (*European 2020 Ecommerce Regional Report*, 2021, p. 34). European e-commerce was worth €717 billion at the end of 2020, with a 12 percent growth that shows signs of a year-on-year slow-down. Central and Eastern Europe (CEE) is the region where the largest growth in digital transformation has been recorded in recent years.

Since the interpretations of CEE countries differ, in this Element we use the definition established by the United Nations Statistics Division, which has a list of geographic regions it uses in its publications and databases. According to this interpretation, CEE consists of: Belarus, Bulgaria, the Czech Republic, Hungary, Poland, the Republic of Moldova, Romania, Russia, Slovakia, and Ukraine (*United Nations Group of Experts on Regional Names*, 2021).

The e-commerce markets in Romania and Bulgaria both increased by 30 percent in 2020, which is the highest growth number in Europe. These, however, are also the two countries with the lowest share of online shoppers (31 and 29 percent respectively). Russia stands out in the region as an e-retail powerhouse, with e-commerce growing ten times faster than traditional retail (*Eastern and Central Europe on Payment Trends*, 2020). The growth potential of CEE digital shopping is also visible in the pace of mobile retail commerce sales growth in 2021 in CEE. The region noted the second highest growth rank (behind Latin America) of 22.3 percent (*Retail mCommerce Sales Growth Worldwide*, 2021).

Importantly, the CEE region is not a consistent one in terms of digital and e-commerce adoption. With growing internet penetration in each of the CEE countries and major leaps observed both in e-commerce and m-commerce adoption, the region should be treated as one with significant potential for growth, with globalization of digital consumer behaviors and growing consumer confidence being significant factors that underline the potential of the region. Indeed, the COVID-19 pandemic has only accelerated digital transition and has helped to bring populations closer to e-commerce, including in countries that were previously slower to adopt new shopping technologies.

The CEE region's development in e-commerce seems to be a battleground between, on the one hand, the globalization of consumer expectations and, on the other, geo-political barriers and dependencies. In some countries, consumers' enthusiasm towards digital technologies appears to indicate the market's strong readiness for e-commerce development. For example, Polish consumers are among the fastest in Europe to transition to digital wallets, and Romanians are the top consumers of mobile technologies. On the other hand, low levels of trust make Ukrainians and Russians wary of digital payments, meaning that physical payment remains the most popular form of transaction (Sergi, 2019). These contrasting forces create a unique digital landscape, which makes CEE a region that can experience sustained growth based on digitization.

1 Systematic Literature Review of Digital Innovation in Emerging Markets of Central and Eastern Europe

The economies of Central and Eastern Europe have been a focus of research since the early 1990s, when they showed record growth and progress after decades of socialism. However, this unprecedented growth was achieved while relying on structures created by the politics of the Soviet bloc, which bear unique implications on the shape of the countries today. Szunomár (2020) outlines the geo-political specifics of the region regarding the countries' shared approach towards innovation during the Soviet era. The political and economic development of CEE countries took shape under the Soviet totalitarian regime of omnipotent bureaucratic coordination in the economy (Szunomár, 2020, p. 22). The system favored concentration of industries and the establishment of large, vertical companies. Under such conditions, innovations were treated as uncertain and threatening, and therefore redundant. Szunomár also claims that "engineering and research capacities were used to innovate around already existing technical solutions of the West" (Szunomár, 2020, p. 23). Most companies in the Soviet bloc performed poorly and lacked modern knowledge of business management. International cooperation was undesirable and sometimes even forbidden, with the state controlling all foreign contact.

Socialist countries were not uniform though, with Poland and Hungary attempting to introduce political and economic reforms after 1989 that impacted upon the logic of their centrally planned economies and opened the countries up towards market-driven Western economic systems. However, such an approach was significantly different from other CEE countries that had belonged to the Soviet bloc. Szanyi and Szabo (2020) state that the development gap increased especially after the oil shocks of 1970s and the transformational crisis after the collapse of Soviet-style economies occurred throughout the region, causing further losses in economic output. Nolke and Vliegenthart state that "since the collapse of state socialism in the late 1980s, the Czech Republic, Hungary,

Poland, and the Slovak Republic have introduced a rather successful model of capitalism when compared with other post-socialist states" (Nolke and Vliegenthart, 2009). Szunomár (2020) supports this opinion by stating that "the four Visegrad countries (Poland, Czechia, Slovakia and Hungary – V4) had always been relatively more developed than the Balkan countries (Romania, Bulgaria, Serbia), and also their transition process seemed to be more consequent and quicker" (Szunomár, 2020, p. 25).

Privatization of state-owned businesses and new labor reforms in Bulgaria, Croatia, the Czech Republic, Hungary, Poland, Romania, and Slovakia followed and opened the markets to foreign investments. However, after the initial years of economic development, a decline in CEE economies occurred until the mid-1990s with recessions lasting until the early 2000s (and even longer in the Balkans), followed by very rapid development and a massive influx of multinational businesses. As observed by Szanyi (2021), these accelerating trends were still not sufficient to match leading European economies, even in the V4 countries (Szanyi, 2021, p. 68). Insufficient acceleration was a result of exceptionally slow development of the 1974–90 period.

The global financial crisis of 2008 again put a halt to rapid growth of CEE economies. However, after subsequent recession, the region's economies reverted to the pace of annual growth rates that had allowed them to advance and chase Western-European economies. With an average GDP growth of 3.9 percent between 2015 and 2017, CEE markets developed 70 percent faster than Western Europe and more than twice as fast as the European Union's "Big 5" of France, Germany, Italy, Spain, and the United Kingdom (*Real GDP Growth Rate,* 2020).

As observed by Labaye (2013), economic models of CEE markets need to be adapted to underline investment-led growth that is focused on digitization, infrastructure improvements, accelerated urbanization, regulatory reforms, institution building, investments in labor-force skills, and efforts to encourage R&D and innovation. In addition, these economies must address the aging of the workforce by raising the labor-participation rate of women and younger workers (Labaye, 2013, p. 29).

In 2019, before data including the COVID-19 pandemic impacted forecasts, Novak et al. (2019) stated that "by closing the digital gap to Western and Northern Europe, CEE could earn up to EUR 200 billion in additional GDP by 2025" (Novak et al., 2019, p. 9). Digitization, they argue, would secure this scenario by digital transformation of public and private sectors, and by boosting e-commerce.

Linked to this, Namysł et al. (2019) also consider e-commerce as the key trend in European retail, with considerable room for growth, especially in mobile commerce (Namysł, Jurkanis, Yearwood, and Sikora, 2019, p. 3). According to 2019 forecasts, m-commerce was estimated to take 27 percent of total e-commerce in Europe by 2022 (Namysł, Jurkanis, Yearwood, and Sikora, 2019, p. 3).

Pre-COVID-19 predictions assumed a continuous process of globalization and developing integration between European countries. Cross-border e-commerce and multinational digital transformation were at the core of the forecasted shifts in favor of CEE countries. Development of information technologies in CEE brought new forms of business organization, where more mature markets could integrate their operations with a lower-cost labor force and growing digital expertise. As stated by Szanyi (2021), "the CEE countries become primarily as innovation and human suppliers of global firms" (Szanyi, 2021, p. 69).

However, these new forms of cooperation are bringing shifts to value chains and the loss of autonomy in decision making (Yakovlev, 2021, p. 34). New markets, including those of CEE, began to pose a threat to existing players, making the opportunities of business integration less optimistic. Yakovlev (2021) predicts "a fresh increase in polarization between rich and poor countries" (Yakovlev, 2021, p. 34).

Moreover, longstanding and viable technology development programs require the development of competitive local companies. Economies in CEE still struggle with stable, local technological performance due to deep-seated corruption and rent seeking, which blocks innovation (Szanyi, 2021, p. 69). Lack of systemic change in a competition-based economy may lead to insufficient development of local digital competition and decreasing integration with multinational technology companies. Szanyi (2021) also sees risks for CEE from China's emerging economy, which could destabilize the competitive edge of CEE, and create unsustainable dependence on Chinese investments and technologies (Szanyi, 2021, pp. 72–3).

Technological development and innovation in e-commerce are key drivers for CEE e-commerce to grow and build a competitive edge (Novak et al., 2019, p. 42). Technical progress has been treated as the "introduction of new processes that reduce the cost of producing an essentially unchanged product" (Rosenberg, 1983, p. 4). Technical progress, according to Rosenberg (1983), should always be supplemented by product innovation, which drives quality improvement and is "the most important long-term contribution of technical progress to human welfare" (Rosenberg, 1983, p. 4).

There is a common agreement among leading CEE market analysts and forecasters that the region is well positioned to propel technology development and innovation. Reports by Galante et al. (2013), Manyjka et al. (2016),

Ignatowicz et al. (2018), and Namysł et al. (2019) all give a comprehensive outlook on CEE digital evolution and potential. The e-commerce surge caused by the COVID-19 pandemic in 2020 only strengthened the optimistic market predictions, which can be observed in the works of Dan (2021a, b, c, d), Khoruzhyy (2021), Milasevic (2021), Poletajevas (2021) and Iszkowska et al. (2021). E-commerce, together with mobile e-commerce, are unanimously considered the top drivers for growth and the top priorities for innovation in CEE.

One of the prevalent factors driving digital transformation forward is the way CEE's citizens have embraced the shift. Beugelsdijk et al. (2017) underline that there are specific cultural traits that can be more region than country-specific, which allows us to treat the CEE as a cultural cluster (Beugelsdijk et al., 2017, p. 35). This supra-national cultural unity is possible since "countries having a history of close ties because of proximity, trade, conquest or religion show more similar cultural values due to institutional transmission than do countries lacking such ties" (Peterson and Barreto, 2015, p. 26). Tsiotsou (2019) uses Hofstede's six cultural value score model to outline the specifics of the CEE cluster, stating that "Central Eastern European countries are high in power distance, uncertainty avoidance, collectivism, long-term orientation and restraint" (Tsiotsou, 2019, p. 825). Solomon et al. (2010) define "emerging consumer culture" – to which CEE states adhere – as one that is defined by rapid change and aspirational shopping behaviors due to exposure to global communication and external market pressure (Solomon, Bamossy, Askegaard, and Hogg, 2010, p. 48). The level to which CEE consumers strive to mimic Western consumer patterns is debated by de Mooij (2018), who raises the argument of nationalism and price-driven rational shopping as a contrast to Western impact on CEE (de Mooij, 2018, p. 33). Arnold et al. (2019) also draw attention to lower purchasing power of CEE consumers as an important factor affecting their purchasing decision-making process (Arnold, Chadraba, and Springer, 2019, p. 8).

Most recent predictions about further digital transformation of the CEE region are focused mainly on consumer-driven digital readiness and trends propelled by the COVID-19 pandemic and do not elaborate on the systemic issues voiced by Szanyi (2021) or Yakovlev (2021). Högselius (2005) claims that due to CEE's economic and societal legacy, future development of the region can only be achieved via "active involvement in the creative generation and further development of . . . new technological processes" (Högselius, 2005, p. 3), and not with one-to-one imitation and adaptation of Western formats. The economic strengths of CEE so far have mainly been found in areas where competitiveness is determined by the availability of low-wage labor, whereas innovation came from the Western markets (Sergi, Bagatelas, and Kubicova,

2007; Högselius, 2005, p. 5). Creative innovation in digital and e-commerce can break this pattern if it is driven by markets themselves and if it is adapted to local specifics of the CEE cultural cluster (Kucia et al., 2021).

Whether such market-driven innovation would be led by multinational or local enterprises is a matter for debate (Wamboye, Tochkov, and Sergi, 2015). Pfirrmann and Walter (2002) argue that SMEs (small and medium-sized enterprises) could lead successful innovation in the CEE region (Pfirrmann and Walter, 2002, p. 3), whilst Ignatowicz et al. (2018) draw attention to the recent emergence of digital "unicorns" – small local companies that have successfully leveraged the digital economy (Ignatowicz et al., 2018, p. 39). Bitzer (2000) however suggests that since Western models cannot be applied due to different financial and institutional conditions, new models should be created which would consider existing limitations (Bitzer, 2000, p. 23). Ignatowicz et al. (2018) outline seven key enablers for digitization of the CEE region:

- increase of adoption of digital tools
- increase of adoption of digital skills and take-up of digital skills by general population
- development and promotion of digitized government solutions
- leveraging CEE's specialist IT pool
- increase of lifelong learning among individuals and digital trainings by companies
- fostering entrepreneurship to stimulate the start-up ecosystem
- improvement and standardization of CEE regulatory environment to ensure attractiveness of investments and easy scalability across the region (Ignatowicz et al., 2018, p. 42).

In an online addendum to the report created by Ignatowicz et al. in 2018 for McKinsey & Company, Marciniak et al. (2021) share an update on the forecasted growth of CEE digitization and e-commerce. The unlocked potential of digital shopping drew double-digit increases in this sector across all markets in the region, but also put additional pressure on small and medium-sized enterprises, which lag on digital adoption in comparison to bigger and international e-commerce businesses (Marciniak et al., 2021).

Galante et al. underline that recognizing market-specific online user experience is fundamental for successful digitization and e-commerce (Galante, Garcia Lopez, and Monroe, 2013, p. 28). For local players, whether big or small, shopper convenience should be at the core of innovation, and it should always be correlated with quality, product range, and pricing strategy. Value propositions should be adapted to meet current consumer needs, recognizing their shifting behaviors and purchase barriers.

2 The Rise of Digital Shopping in CEE Countries – A Consumer-Led Transformation

Central and Eastern Europe is a 172 million-strong consumer market and, according to Colliers International report, it is poised to deliver better growth rates and returns in retail than most developed markets (Turpin et al., 2021, p. 4). The labor market has been improving steadily for the last decade, in turn increasing purchasing power of consumers. The biggest impact and potential of CEE retail has been e-commerce, which has become fundamental to the transformation of the sector. This impact on online shopping has been even more significant due to the COVID-19 pandemic.

Not all countries have been affected equally by the pandemic and the CEE region recorded circa 1,400 cases per million inhabitants, significantly less than Western Europe (Iszkowska et al., 2021, p. 15). Although these differences can be attributed to lower levels of testing in the region, CEE countries did implement lockdown measures, border closures, mandatory masks outdoors, restrictions on non-essential services, and limitations on social gatherings relatively early and fast.

Strict lockdowns caused abrupt closures of brick-and-mortar stores and long-term disruptions to services. COVID-19 caused a steep 20–45 percent decline in footfall figures in shopping centers in 2020, compared to 2019 (Turpin et al., 2021, p. 9). Even though the share of online sales varies considerably, an e-commerce surge can be observed across the entire CEE region and this shift has occurred because of two, interconnected significant factors – technology and consumers.

Technology in CEE has a strong potential to chase the long-established digital ecosystems of Western Europe. New players in CEE did not suffer such a strong "technology lock-in" as their Western and Northern European counterparts. While more advanced companies in Europe developed their core IT systems during the 1970s and 1980s, CEE countries were neither able to create their own solutions nor to build on Western developments at that time. However, by joining the digitization process relatively late, CEE markets are much less limited by legacy systems that often remain in place in Western markets. Current adoption of new technologies is easier and cheaper for CEE markets, allowing them to leapfrog to the most immediate and most recent technological solutions.

Bypassing technology lock-in puts CEE markets at the forefront of innovation. This can be observed in the fact that the region has seen vibrant growth, with multiple digital success stories across the area, and several digital-native companies achieving unicorn status (a valuation of more than $1 billion)

(Ignatowicz et al., 2018, p. 6). Iszkowska et al. (2021) observe that "various tech clusters are emerging on a regional and country level, strengthening the credibility – and visibility – of specific sectors and individual players on the international stage" (Iszkowska et al., 2021, p. 22). In 2019, among the analyzed markets were five CEE unicorns: Allegro and CD Projekt from Poland, UiPath and eMag from Romania, and Avast from the Czech Republic. There are also numerous rising stars – defined by Iszkowska et al. as non-acquired, non-public start-ups founded since 2000, with a minimum €1 million in total funding and with a maximum valuation of €800 million (Iszkowska et al., 2021, p. 23). Among the analyzed countries, there were twenty-three rising stars in 2019:

- Poland: Applica, Booksy, Brainly, Docplanner, Huuuge, Imfermedica, Nomagic, Packhelp
- Hungary: Almotive, Prezi, Tresorit, Bitrise, Commsignia, Sharp 3D
- Romania: Elefant.ro
- The Czech Republic: Twisto, Liftago
- Bulgaria: Remix, Gtmhub, Office RnD
- Slovakia: Sli.co, Photoneo, Minit.

Most emerging companies operate in the gaming, cybersecurity, software, and fintech sectors. Due to the small size of individual markets in CEE, numerous start-ups do not receive sufficient funding and governmental support to grow and gain international recognition. However, the success of the above examples proves the potential of CEE players. With the COVID-19 pandemic, the European Commission has strengthened its stance on the importance of digital innovation and digital autonomy. Currently CEE countries have a unique opportunity to obtain funds and support for digital transition (Iszkowska et al., 2021, p. 28).

Advancement of CEE in digital economy would not have been possible without the readiness of consumers to embrace the new technologies. Growing connectivity has unlocked new opportunities related to internet usage and reinforced economic growth. Between 2005 and 2014, cross-border bandwidth grew forty-five times and contributed to increasing global GDP by around 3.6 percent (Manyjka, 2016, p. 3). Fast broadband allows CEE societies to benefit from digitization and is fundamental to ensure sustainable development. In this regard, the CEE region is well positioned: over the past twenty years, CEE countries have managed to develop an average of 94 percent household coverage for fixed broadband, very close to the 98 percent benchmark for Western Europe (Manyjka, 2016, p. 31).

Connectivity is the first step for online consumer adoption. Nevertheless, CEE consumers still perform fewer digital activities than their Western counterparts. Online banking is used by 52 percent fewer citizens in the East, with only 39 percent of the population. Using online travel and accommodation services is declared by only 29 percent of the respondents, while in Western Europe this is a practice performed by over half of the population (Ignatowicz et al., 2018, p. 44).

Furthermore, up until recently people in CEE countries have exhibited a relatively low propensity for online spending, at around 15 percent of the US level (Ignatowicz et al., 2018, p. 14). A significant reason for these discrepancies has been considered to lie in a low degree of cross-border e-commerce in Europe: less than 10 percent of firms in the European Union engaged in cross-border sales or purchases in 2019 (Ignatowicz et al., 2018, p. 57). This is not common practice among European consumers, with only one in five Europeans purchasing goods online outside their home market. Consequently, this number is lower in CEE, where only one in ten consumers practice cross-border e-commerce. Ignatowicz et al. (2018, p. 57) state that strong consumer barriers lie behind such low levels of cross-border e-commerce, such as websites in foreign languages, longer delivery times, and higher delivery and return costs. However, it should be added that a surge in new e-commerce retailers, including cross-border giants like Amazon and Alibaba, is gradually opening new opportunities to CEE users with translated websites, attractive prices, and shortened delivery times.

The outbreak of the COVID-19 pandemic caused serious disruption in the functioning of the economies of CEE countries. Lockdowns, forced isolation, closure of retail and service establishments, sports venues, cultural establishments, etc. were traumatic experiences for many consumers, especially among the younger cohorts of the population. Consumers in many countries, including the CEE region, changed their everyday routine behaviors overnight (Mróz, 2021a, p. 36).

The 2020 COVID-19 pandemic drastically reshaped the global e-commerce landscape, leading to the biggest growth of e-commerce share across the entire CEE region. The unprecedented spread of the virus and subsequent lockdowns brought about new consumer needs and habits and, consequently, new solutions from businesses who struggled to survive in the changing environment. Closed shopping centers and home seclusion resulted in a sharp drop in sales in brick-and-mortar retail outlets and boosted a rapid increase in turnover in online stores, which began to experience a real surge, and the waiting time for delivery of ordered goods increased several fold (Mróz, 2021a, p. 41).

During the first months of the COVID-19 lockdowns, the digital economy of CEE accelerated considerably, "capturing 78%, or EUR 5.3 billion, of the increase seen in the whole of 2019 within the space of just five months" (Marciniak et al., 2021). The e-commerce surge has been driven mainly by unprecedented consumer demand. Since the early months of 2020, 15 percent more consumers have accessed at least one online service in CEE. Before the pandemic, CEE users accessed around two services online daily, but this number doubled in 2020 (Novak et al., 2021).

Despite declining business activity, growing unemployment, and economic turmoil, the region has observed an unprecedented level of digitization, led by changing shopper behaviors. Consumers were offered a broader selection of online services, resulting in more extensive usage of digital solutions.

Research on the impact of the COVID-19 pandemic on CEE consumers performed by Iszkowska et al. (2021) shows that all age groups and geographies underwent a rapid digital adoption. Eighty-eight percent of consumers who accessed digital services said that they were either "satisfied" or "very satisfied" with the service (Iszkowska et al., 2021, p. 38). The main sources of dissatisfaction were the difficulty of using digital services and a lack of a full range of products accessible online (Iszkowska et al., 2021, p. 38). Importantly, across Europe as a whole almost 70 percent of users admitted that they would be willing to continue using digital services at the same or an even higher level after the pandemic (Iszkowska et al., 2021, p. 38). It means that private and public sectors should support the digital transformation of the economy to adapt to the new consumer behaviors.

One of the noteworthy consumer trends in the virtual environment is social commerce. Social media during the COVID-19 pandemic have become a catalyst for e-commerce development in CEE countries. Young adult consumers treat the Internet as a space where they can relax and entertain themselves, but also build bonds with other users as well as get valuable inspiration, tips, and advice. For self-assured, empowered consumers in CEE, the Web is also a place where they can share opinions on products and resolve their shopping dilemmas with the help of other users (Mróz, 2021b).

Reinforcing consumers' readiness towards a digital economy should be at the core of CEE digitization and building a strong talent pool of digital experts could reinforce digital infrastructure and further develop internet coverage. Furthermore, governments and businesses should digitize their offerings, by making consumer journeys more convenient and simpler. Customer needs shifted towards online channels since the COVID-19 pandemic outbreak, and therefore product offerings should be adapted.

3 Key Shopper Behaviors and Drivers across CEE Markets

The CEE region has a social and economic legacy that brings as many challenges as opportunities to its population. Cultural differences and the stage of consumer society evolution create differences in attitudes to shopping (Hedley, 2007). At the same time, even though the CEE region faces economic and technological challenges, its population has access to digital media and global utilities. The key challenge is at what pace consumers in CEE will adapt to and embrace the new technologies.

3.1 CEE Consumer Culture

Despite promising trends and impressive 2020 growth, consumers in CEE countries differ significantly from their Western-European counterparts in terms of digital skills. Ignatowicz et al. estimate that only 47 percent of the CEE population aged between sixteen and seventy-four have basic digital skills, in comparison to 70 percent of the Western-European population. The same research also points to a considerably lower usage of the Internet overall (77 percent of the population, against 93 percent in Western Europe) (Ignatowicz et al., 2018, p. 44).

Consequently, only 57 percent of CEE internet users perform internet research and only 62 percent send emails. These data shed light on a discrepancy between digital connectivity and digital adoption in CEE (Ignatowicz et al., 2018, p. 44). Also, in the analyzed region younger populations act as the early adopters of technology. Tech-savvy Millennials and Gen Z-ers perceive the Web and social networking platforms as a space offering attractive consumer experiences. It can be assumed that cutting-edge, disruptive technologies will intensify the process and serve as a catalyst for development of e-commerce on digital platforms in the coming years (Harji, 2021; Martinez-Ruiz and Moser, 2019; Mróz, 2021b). However, broader adoption across entire populations is still needed to facilitate the growth of the digital economy.

The purchasing power of CEE consumers remains the lowest across Europe, which directly affects their openness to digital shopping. In a 2020 study performed by GfK, Moldova and Ukraine recorded the lowest purchasing power index, while the Czech Republic, one of the highest-ranking countries in the region, had a per capita purchasing power of €9,179, which puts it almost 34 percent below the European average and in twenty-fifth place among the forty-two countries in the study (*Europeans Have Around EUR 773 Less in 2020 Due to COVID-19*, 2021).

Even though lower digitization and purchasing power affect how CEE consumers shop, the population is also a part of a global consumer culture that unites people by "their common devotion to brand-name consumer goods, film stars and rock stars" (Solomon, Bamossy, Askegaard, and Hogg, 2010, p. 14). Popular culture and consumer trends have a global and unifying impact that is facilitated by digital connectivity and social media. Consumer needs evolve globally as products and services from different geographies and cultures mix and merge (Aslam and Azhar, 2013; Revinova, 2019). Therefore, consumers remain interconnected and impact themselves as much as businesses.

Three decades of transition towards market economy in CEE triggered far-reaching consequences for various spheres of social, economic, and political life in CEE countries including changes in consumption patterns and consumer behaviors. Shopping queues and chronic shortages of necessities became vague memories of the past. Consumers in CEE countries found themselves in a "global village" under strong pressure of patterns of consumption typical of cosmopolitan consumer culture (Mróz, 2013).

However, consumers in the CEE region have a particular relationship with global consumerism. Termed by Solomon et al. (2010) as an "emerging consumer culture," it is defined by rapid changes in social, political, and economic dimensions to fit the resources to the sudden exposure to global communication and external market pressure (Solomon, Bamossy, Askegaard, and Hogg, 2010, p. 48). It seems that the young generations of CEE consumers are, for the most part, fascinated with the global consumer culture and responsive to the lure of related behavioral patterns: they eagerly buy products and gadgets that attest that they belong to the global "tribe of consumers." The same attitude to the cosmopolitan global culture is taken by people with high consumer aspirations, oriented to rivalry, social prestige, and financial status. But since a fast transition to fit the global models is unattainable for most of the population, relatively large segments of CEE societies start expressing a loss of confidence and pride in local culture. As a result, CEE consumers have a specific yearning towards Western culture and products that is unfulfilled due to a lasting economic gap.

However, de Mooij (2018) observes that with gradually improved quality and lower prices of local CEE brands, consumers are more and more eager to shop for local offerings (de Mooij, 2018, p. 33). This gradual shift is facilitated by growing nationalism and a greater proximity of brands' narrative to local values. CEE consumers have a specific set of needs, which makes their consumer behaviors differ from those of their Western-European neighbors. Their decision-making process is more rational and prolonged – an effect of lower purchasing power and stronger focus on price competitiveness (Escribano and Pena, 2021; Arnold, Chadraba, and Springer, 2019, p. 8). They also have a rather critical attitude to a purely lifestyle-based communication – often implemented in Western advertising strategies – and are more prone to trust brands with feature-driven, informative communication (Arnold, Chadraba, and Springer, 2019, p. 9). This need is in line with general consumer mistrust, which is often attributed to the stigma over poor local product quality and ongoing corruption in numerous business segments. The same pattern is also expressed in the lasting popularity of cash-on-delivery payments in e-commerce, which is a specific trait of the CEE digital landscape.

3.2 COVID-19 Consumer Shift

Even though the shift to digitalized shopping behaviors has been developing for the past decade, it is undeniably the 2020 COVID-19 pandemic that propelled mass digital adoption in CEE markets. The pandemic has had a profound impact on consumer behaviors and forced businesses to readjust their approach. During 2020 over 12 million new users of online services appeared in CEE (Marciniak, 2021). What is notable about this surge is the age of the new users. Until 2020, online usage has mainly been the domain of younger consumers, but during the pandemic the biggest growth, of 40 percent, was observed among consumers aged over sixty-five (Marciniak, 2021).

Indeed, CEE e-commerce growth in 2020 has been one of the most impressive across the entire digital sector. The number of consumers using online channels for entertainment and grocery shopping doubled and grew up to 70 percent for retail (Novak et al., 2021). As per Kohli et al., the year 2020 brought "a decade in days in adoption of digital" (Kohli et al., 2020, p. 2).

The COVID-19 pandemic had a significant impact on people's lives and consumer behaviors, spanning multiple areas of life, which collectively impact upon how consumers perceive their needs, barriers, and purchasing patterns. Even though the shifts have been rapid, they are likely to have an important, and possibly lasting, effect on how retailers and manufacturers should plan for the years to come. However, behavioral changes are not linear, and their chances of being permanent will depend on how consumers embrace the new experiences (Kohli et al., 2020, p. 6). Kohli et al. (2020) outline the following consumer macro-trends that can affect shopping and consumption long-term:

- consumer shift towards online shopping
- preference for trusted brands
- decline in discretionary spending and trading down
- polarization of sustainability (Kohli et al., 2020, p. 6).

The above-mentioned trends will have an impact on the entire consumer journey, bringing a lasting shift to how consumers discover brands, what they decide to buy, and where they finalize their purchases. Many consumers have been forced to leapfrog towards e-commerce, building a lasting expectation of a more seamless omnichannel experience. The same behaviors can be observed in the CEE region, where consumers faced lockdowns and major limitations to their usual shopping behaviors (Poletajevas, 2021b). E-retailers quickly adapted to the changing needs by expanding their online product assortments through groceries (i.e. Wildberries in Russia and Allegro in Poland) and assuring faster delivery thanks to increased operations through new logistics centers. The notorious mistrust towards online payments has been mitigated by secure-payment partnerships and the new market entries of Apple Pay and Google Pay.

The already price-conscious mindset of CEE consumers was further strengthened by the financial uncertainty of the COVID-19 pandemic. Poletajevas highlights that even while economic indicators improved, "consumer spending habits were slower to evolve, partially due to a low level of trust in banks" (Poletajevas, 2021b). Frugal consumers flocked to cheaper solutions offered by foreign players in e-commerce, which signals a growing eagerness of CEE shoppers to choose foreign products if they remain a cheaper alternative to local brands.

The trends outlined in CEE consumer behaviors show an increasing urgency for businesses to adapt their offerings to this challenging market, which is driven by growing demand for convenience and price-competitiveness. However, a broader context of these shifts can only be provided by analysis of CEE markets' performance.

4 CEE E-Commerce Market Deep Dive

Looking at Europe from the perspective of digitization and e-commerce, Ignatowicz et al. (2018) distinguish three broad groups of countries. The most advanced group in their analysis is of relatively small countries with very high digitization rates: Belgium, Denmark, Estonia, Finland, Ireland, Luxembourg, the Netherlands, Norway, and Sweden. The second one, the EU Big 5, before Brexit consisted of France, Germany, Italy, Spain, and the United Kingdom. The third group covers CEE countries: Bulgaria, Croatia, the Czech Republic, Hungary, Latvia, Lithuania, Poland, Romania, Slovakia, and Slovenia (Ignatowicz et al., 2018, p. 5).

Since the interpretations of CEE countries differ, in this Element the authors use the definition established by the United Nations Statistics Division, which has a list of geographic regions it uses in its publications and databases. According to this interpretation, CEE consists of Belarus, Bulgaria, the Czech Republic, Hungary, Poland, the Republic of Moldova, Romania, Russia, Slovakia, and Ukraine (*United Nations Group of Experts on Regional Names*, 2021).

Since the early 1990s, CEE countries have enjoyed significant economic growth. Gross domestic product (GDP) per capita grew by 114 percent between

1996 and 2017 and the main growth drivers during this period were traditional industries, dynamic exports, investments from abroad, labor-cost advantages, and funding from the European Union (Ignatowicz et al., 2018, p. 10). However, the speed of growth is now slowing down, and CEE remains undercapitalized in comparison to other European economies. Existing growth models based on the combination of low labor costs, exports, and capital inflows through foreign direct investments are reaching their limits and are "less and less capable to propel the engine of economic convergence" (Geberen and Wruuck, 2021, p. 8).

CEE labor costs are three to four times lower than in other countries, with an average hourly wage of €10 (Iszkowska et al., 2021, p. 15). The exemplary wage difference of €39 per hour between Denmark and Bulgaria shows that even with a fast increase of labor costs, CEE would need more than a decade to reach the level of labor costs of Western European countries.

The capital stock (total gross fixed assets per employee) is on average 60 percent lower in CEE than for the most-developed economies of EU Member States. This means that CEE countries have a significantly lower capability to automate the manual labor. This major gap has been covered by high availability of an inexpensive workforce that could make up for losses in automation and productivity.

However, workforce costs are also rising, and labor reserves are declining, with unemployment in CEE at record low levels. Moreover, the inflow of EU funds to CEE countries is likely to weaken after 2020 (Ignatowicz et al., 2018, p. 10).

Intensified digital transformation and innovation could strengthen the position of the region and accelerate its pace of growth. It can be observed however that the digital economy of CEE has developed very unevenly, not only in respective countries, but also in respective sectors. The sectors exhibiting the highest digitization rates are information and communication technologies (ICT), finance, and insurance. The second group also includes large sectors, such as manufacturing and wholesale retail trades. The sectors closest to the consumer market, such as entertainment, accommodation, food services, health care, and education are at the lowest level of CEE digitization rates (Ignatowicz et al., 2018, p. 16). This notwithstanding, it can be observed that the COVID-19 pandemic disrupted the markets and brought significant progress in multiple e-commerce sectors, giving an optimistic outline into future development of digital economy in CEE region.

4.1 Belarus

With a population of nearly 10 million, Belarus is an emerging consumer market with a growing e-commerce sector. The COVID-19 pandemic boosted e-commerce sales value, recording growth of 38 percent in 2020 (Khoruzhyy, 2021a). E-commerce sales are expected to rise at a steadier, but still double-digit value, reaching BYN 6.3 billion (circa €2.1 billion) in 2025.

Consumer behaviors in Belarus have shifted considerably due to the COVID-19 pandemic, even though the government did not impose a lockdown. Nevertheless, in their attempt to avoid personal contact, shoppers turned to online purchases of groceries and everyday necessities, such as personal care and home care products. These categories, together with consumer electronics, contributed the most to the strong e-commerce growth in 2020.

The food and drink e-commerce platforms, e-dostavka.by and gipermail.by, became significant players thanks to their wide assortment, fast delivery, and low minimum order.

The success of E-dostavka.by is due to its wide national coverage, offering delivery not only to larger cities, but also to villages.

Despite the success of local players, foreign e-commerce platforms have a significant presence in Belarus, with the third-party merchant Alibaba Group Holding having the leading value share in 2020, attracting 21 percent of online shoppers. Alibaba offers a broad range of inexpensive products on the AliExpress e-commerce platform. In Belarus, licensing of imported products is mandatory, making small items sold in Belarus expensive compared to Chinese offerings. Cross-border e-commerce, especially Chinese, can thus thrive in Belarus thanks to lower prices, wide product variety, and ongoing improvements in consumer experience and delivery options. In 2020 AliExpress partnered with the local Alfa-bank to offer a dedicated debit card with cashback for purchases on the platform. This type of incentive is an effective mechanism to nurture loyalty towards a single platform among consumers willing to receive bonuses for their purchases.

Another consumer-driven shift in Belarus can be observed with the growing number of mobile e-commerce purchases. Especially in the first months of the COVID-19 pandemic, shoppers bought more smartphones as the availability of attractive installment payments grew (Khoruzhyy, 2021b). In addition, mobile internet subscriptions increased thanks to affordable mobile internet offerings. Another factor that boosted e-mobile commerce is the introduction of Apple Pay to Belarus and the launch of the Huawei/Honor mobile application allowing mobile payments. Both events took place in 2020, facilitating consumer adoption of mobile payment methods in the country. Government control over all in-country mobile payments allows for high confidence in new mobile payment options.

Consequently, consumers switched to their smartphones to browse and shop essential products on both local websites and foreign e-retailers, who have a bigger scale and the financial opportunities to build sophisticated mobile applications and who thus offer stern competition to local companies. The AliExpress mobile application is available in Russian, including comments and feedback, which, combined with competitive prices, attracts a growing number of Belarusians not only to the desktop version of the website, but also to the app.

Nevertheless, the COVID-19 pandemic in Belarus unlocked new opportunities for local businesses in e-commerce. Leading offline players opened their online platforms with cash-on-delivery payment methods (unavailable for foreign players) and in-store pick-up options. This is a very bold move and an opportunity for local players, given that the most popular online payment methods in Belarus are cash on delivery, followed by credit card and e-wallets (*Selling online in Belarus,* 2020).

These features are also of major importance since e-commerce opportunities in Belarus are being hampered by high delivery costs. With the liquidation of GloBel24, one of the country's leading providers, in 2020, the number of players decreased, and its departure had a considerable impact on the attractiveness of local e-commerce offerings in the country. A further limitation on the e-commerce surge in Belarus is the lack of permits for sale of specific product categories, such as jewelry and pharmaceuticals. However, with a temporary lift of the ban for online pharmaceuticals sales in 2020, further changes are expected, which will encourage continuous development of e-commerce.

Despite the political instability of Belarus and its subsequent economic downturn in 2020, consumer spending is still expected to see double-digit growth in 2021 and beyond (Khoruzhyy, 2021a).

4.2 Bulgaria

Bulgaria is the sixty-sixth largest export economy in the world and the thirty-seventh most complex economy according to the Economic Complexity Index (*E-Commerce in Bulgaria,* 2020). With a population of 7 million, the level of online sales was valued at €690 million in 2018.

The share of online shoppers among internet users is estimated at 35 percent (*The E-Commerce Market in Bulgaria,* 2020). The COVID-19 pandemic was not the only trigger for an e-commerce surge, as was the case in Belarus, but rather a facilitator in a steady and continuous development of this shopping channel (Khoruzhyy, 2021b). Grocery e-commerce was the only exception, with impressive triple-digit growth in 2020, as consumers showed increased demand for this product category (Khoruzhyy, 2021b).

The strong, rapid adoption of grocery shopping online, even if forced by an unprecedented pandemic event and subsequent lockdowns, shows that consumer shopping behaviors are steadily shifting towards e-commerce. Still, a vast majority of consumers in Bulgaria prefer to pay cash on delivery for their online purchases, accounting for a 70 percent share of all purchases (*E-Commerce in Bulgaria*, 2020).

It has been predicted that the compound annual growth rate (CAGR) of e-commerce for the next four years will be 16 percent. Compared to the year-on-year growth of 41 percent, this decrease suggests a moderately flooded market. Another indicator of market saturation is the online penetration of 35 percent in Bulgaria; in other words, 35 percent of the population bought at least one product online in 2020. The channel is set to continue taking market share from offline grocery retailers, which will contribute the most to the growth of this channel. The shift from offline non-grocery retail to online is predicted to remain strong but it will not be such a strong driver as online grocery shopping in Bulgaria (Khoruzhyy, 2021b). Major offline grocery players are entering the online market, including Lidl, which will be replicating the omnichannel model introduced in Poland a few years ago.

The biggest player on the Bulgarian e-commerce market is currently eMAG.bg. The store had a revenue of US$52 million in 2020. This is followed by remix-shop.com, with US$37 million revenue, and fashiondays.bg, with US$24 million revenue. Altogether, the top three stores account for 15 percent of online revenue in Bulgaria (*The E-Commerce Market in Bulgaria*, 2020). Other leading online stores include koketna.com, bgfashionzone.com, secretzone.bg, and fashiondays. bg, which proves that fashion is the leading sector of online shopping, accounting for 35 percent of total online sales in the country. This is followed by electronics and media with 29 percent, toys and hobby appliances with 15 percent, furniture and home accessories with 13 percent, and food and personal care with the remaining 8 percent (*The E-Commerce Market in Bulgaria*, 2020).

The store eMAG.bg is not only the e-commerce leader, but also a frontrunner in mobile commerce in Bulgaria. As an early entrant to m-commerce, with a mobile app launched in 2015, eMAG.bg benefited from users' increased shift towards mobile devices during 2020. To further involve shoppers in in-app purchases, the e-retailer organizes mobile-only promotional events, including the globally recognized Black Friday. Other mobile e-commerce players are unable to match the performance of eMAG.bg, and the brand takes the lead for consumers, as well as new market players (Khoruzhyy, 2021d).

Even though Bulgaria's shift towards e-commerce has been upward in recent years, the country had the lowest share of online shoppers in the European Union in 2019. While the pandemic has facilitated the speed of adoption among consumers, the country still requires some regulatory and legal changes if shoppers' expectations are to be met, and the country is still in need of clearer regulation of online sales and data privacy. With these measures taken, the Bulgarian e-commerce market might see continuous growth based on growing consumer trust.

4.3 The Czech Republic

The Czech Republic is one of the leaders in European e-commerce. The number of e-shops per citizen is the highest in Europe, currently at around 40,000 total (*E-Commerce in Czech Republic*, 2021). With the digital boost caused by the COVID-19 pandemic, e-commerce retail value in 2020 rose by 27 percent (Milasevic, 2021). Impressively, e-commerce accounted for around 13.5 percent of the total retail turnover as consumers tried to minimize the number of shopping outlets and chose to buy online across numerous categories, many of which were previously offline-based (*E-Commerce in Czech Republic*, 2021).

Consumer electronics is the leading e-commerce category and throughout 2020 it maintained its winning position. However, the highest growth was recorded in grocery and home appliances, which again reflects the changing lifestyles of consumers, who avoided physical contact throughout the year and spent more time at home. Consequently, pharmaceutical e-commerce also saw a dynamic uplift, especially in the OTC and supplements category (Milasevic, 2021).

Cross-border e-commerce in the Czech Republic is highly influenced by Chinese online marketplaces, which continued their expansion throughout 2020. In the challenging pandemic period, consumers began to accept longer delivery times amid financial uncertainty. The scale of the Chinese impact could be observed based on delivery patterns – most parcels from China are of low value and constitute 70 percent of parcels arriving in the Czech Republic (Milasevic, 2021a). Chinese e-retailers benefit from EU-wide VAT exemption on goods from this country, with all goods with a value of below €22 being excluded from VAT and duty fees.

Despite the considerable maturity of e-commerce in the country, Czech online shoppers favor click-and-collect and in-store payments for their purchases. Still, online and bank transfer payments are forecasted to grow in importance until 2025 (Milasevic, 2021a).

In an already developed Czech e-commerce market, the pandemic spurred further innovations that, in turn, built stronger demand. Alza.cz and Internet Mall, key players in the sector, offered e-retailer platforms and infrastructure to sell goods and broaden product portfolios for merchants struggling with dropping sales. Alza Neo, a subsidiary offering IT equipment rental, saw a surge in demand from businesses opening their online stores (Milasevic, 2021a).

Consumers benefited from contactless click-and-collect features and the pure e-commerce player Zoot introduced their own courier service, which allowed customers to try on clothes and return them to the courier if necessary, saving on postal returns.

Mobile e-commerce in the Czech Republic grew significantly in 2020 amid the COVID-19 pandemic and, although it covered different product and service categories, the rise was most significant in apparel, footwear, electronics, and books (Milasevic, 2021b). Alza.cz declared that around one-third of its customers made orders from mobile devices, proving a trend that is also reflected in the three-digit value growth from Android and iOS apps.

4.4 Hungary

As in other CEE countries, the COVID-19 pandemic in Hungary was the catalyst for increased online shopping, with a 15 percent value increase in 2020 and a further 18 percent increase forecast by 2025 (Dan, 2021a). Numerous domestic in-store retail outlets opened their e-commerce shops to respond to dramatically decreased foot traffic in 2020, but third-party merchants remained key online players, with a value share of 6 percent (Dan, 2021a).

Ongoing lockdowns and the e-commerce surge unlocked opportunities for new product categories, with advanced spending recorded for daily hygiene and sanitary products, home appliances, and gardening accessories (Dan, 2021a). A significant rise in trust in e-commerce could be observed among older consumers and in the entire population of internet users, with an increased proportion of online payments. The shift towards e-commerce is forecasted to remain strong, with continuing growth in new product categories, such as groceries.

The Hungarian e-commerce market is competing with the CEE websites that are continuously extending their cross-border coverage, especially in categories such as beauty, personal care, pet food, and apparel (Dan, 2021a). Strong growth from the local Hungarian market can, however, be observed in mobile e-commerce, which witnessed an impressive value increase of 93 percent in 2020 (Dan, 2021b). The timely launch of the Apple digital wallet in 2020 partly facilitated this rise, which is forecasted to increase further by 34 percent of its current value by 2025 (Dan, 2021b).

4.5 Poland

In 2020 Polish e-commerce recorded a 42 percent retail value growth, with strong leadership by third-party merchants, who accounted for a 38 percent share of the combined retail value (Milasevic, 2021b). As in other CEE countries, the growth can be attributed to the lockdowns necessitated by the COVID-19 pandemic and retailers' stronger focus on digital and omnichannel solutions.

Grupa Allegro is the biggest and most impactful e-retailer and marketplace in Poland, responsible for 65 percent of the Polish e-commerce market and an impressive increase to nearly 18 million active users in 2020 (*Allegro liderem polskiego rynku e-commerce*, 2020). Allegro also benefits from impressive top-of-mind brand awareness in Poland, being the most recognized online brand for 86 percent of consumers (Sass-Staniszewska and Binert, 2020, p. 22). Grupa Allegro's activities have a considerable impact on consumers' adaptation towards e-commerce solutions. In 2020 the company introduced Allegro Pay, a new consumer finance product offering credit lines and flexible payment options. The same year, a special service for seniors was introduced, offering users a dial-in customer service that assisted shoppers through their purchase journey on the platform.

The strength of Allegro as an e-retailer and as a brand has highly disrupted the entrance of Amazon into the Polish market in 2020. Upon overall disappointment with Amazon's entry offering, Allegro's stock rates increased by 5 percent (Hirsh, 2021). However, Amazon is still forecasted to account for 12 percent of the Polish e-commerce market by 2025 (*Amazon, Allegro, e-commerce w Polsce*, 2021).

Besides Allegro, the Polish e-commerce market remains heavily fragmented, with numerous players holding marginal value share (Milasevic, 2021b). Numerous innovations were launched to cater to consumers' changing needs in 2020. Social media has become a significant shopping venue with live broadcast sales, as the one performed by the Quiosque apparel e-retailer in 2020. A majority of scalable and significant innovations have been performed, however, in shipping and delivery solutions. Allegro and Empik – two of Poland's most significant e-commerce players, offered free delivery to Paczkomaty (parcel lockers), and grocery e-retailers opened their omnichannel solutions with click-and-collect options. Empik opened its Premium version to all customers for free during the first months of the pandemic and supported online education by expanding its scholar offering.

Online players began investing in mobile technology, with a stronger focus on developing applications and matching websites to support mobile devices. The COVID-19 pandemic brought about a 48 percent rise in current retail value, with a continued projected growth of 22 percent by 2025 (Milasevic, 2021d).

However, Polish consumers show quite a unique preference for multichannel shopping (in comparison to other analyzed CEE markets). Shoppers tend to combine usage of an e-commerce website, mobile application, and physical store in their purchasing journey. Therefore, smartphones remained mostly used for initial research and price comparison, giving way to desktop e-commerce websites for actual transactions. Mobile devices are used for product research and shopping by 69 percent of Polish shoppers (Sass-Staniszewska and Binert, 2020, p. 203). The importance of mobile e-commerce solutions is even more significant in terms of the speed of technology adoption by the youngest generation, Gen Z. Almost all Polish Gen Z consumers (89 percent) use their mobile devices for research prior to their purchase and they consider smartphones their most important devices (Grabiwoda, 2018, p. 89). The continued popularity of desktop devices used for shopping is maintained mainly by older consumers and this trend will begin to decline in the coming years, as a growing number of user-friendly mobile applications become popularized among shoppers. This trend is already visible on Allegro, where 60 percent of transactions are performed via smartphones and one in three customers made a purchase exclusively via the Allegro app in 2020 (Milasevic, 2021d).

Innovations in e-commerce and omnichannel shopping drive Polish consumers' faster adoption of online purchase methods. Traditional stores are becoming showrooms, which is particularly the case for categories such as apparel and footwear, consumer electronics and appliances, but also homeware and furnishing stores (Milasevic, 2021b). Leading offline retailers, such as Lidl and Rossmann, have focused on the development of mobile applications, which are gaining increasing popularity among Polish shoppers.

Interestingly, Polish e-commerce is forecasted to remain dominated by domestic sales until 2025, driven mainly by the ongoing growth and innovations of Grupa Allegro. The stable position of local e-commerce players is also attributed to the language barrier of Polish consumers (Milasevic, 2021b).

4.6 Moldova

Moldova has the smallest e-commerce market among the analyzed CEE countries, with revenue projected to hit US$148 million by the end of 2021 (Edwards, 2021). The annual growth rate of digital shopping for the last four years has been estimated at 12 percent, however the data for this market is scarce and therefore difficult to measure against other CEE regions.

There are 1.4 million e-commerce shoppers, placing user penetration at 34 percent with a projected increase to 39 percent in 2025 (Edwards, 2021). Fashion is the most shopped category, similar to Bulgaria, another nascent digital economy in the region. Similarly to smaller digital economies, Chinese cross-border commerce is taking a significant piece of the market with inexpensive items and easy payment options. Local e-shops in Moldova are poorly adapted for online payments, while consumers, by shopping online on websites like AliExpress, Amazon, or ASOS are adapting to more innovative and convenient shopping solutions. However, this activity is still small in scale. Only 32 percent of women and 43 percent of men make online transactions and only 17 percent of the population own credit cards (Kemp, 2021). With Google Pay and Apple Pay still unavailable in the country, the transition to mobile commerce will still take some time, although, the popularity of PayPal is beginning to rise.

4.7 Romania

Before the COVID-19 pandemic, Romania was already showing dynamic growth in digital shopping, facilitated by broad penetration of the Internet and advanced consumer adoption of mobile technology. In 2020, Romania saw a 35 percent value growth, with a forecast of a further increase of 18 percent by 2025 (Dan, 2021b). Only 45 percent of Romanian Internet users shopped online in 2019, which puts the country in the bottom three in the European Union, together with Bulgaria and Italy (*Online Shopping Ever More Popular in 2020*, 2021). Romania has, however, recorded the biggest surge in online shoppers in 2020 among all EU countries, followed by the Czech Republic and Hungary (*Online Shopping Ever More Popular in 2020*, 2021).

One of the key factors that changed throughout 2020 and impacted the rapid growth of online shopping was improvement in home delivery services (Dan, 2021b). The initial period of the pandemic increased demand for essential products online to a level that caused massive disruptions and delays.

E-retailers reacted by improving logistics and introducing more permissive return policies, which stabilized the initial disruption and, in effect, created a more convenient and consumer-friendly shopping environment. The leader of digital transformation during the pandemic was eMAG – the biggest market-place and e-retailer in Romania. A marketplace business model allows smaller players to enter the e-commerce market, grow their product portfolio across a single platform and, consequently, broaden their consumer base. The additional business benefit of eMAG is its partnership with International Marketplace Network, which allows sellers to access partner platforms in Germany (Real.de), cDiscount (France), or ePrice (Italy). By the end of 2020 eMAG boasted growth up to 40,000 independent e-retailers on the platform and the number was predicted to grow in 2021 (Dan, 2021b).

The biggest shift in Romania from the consumer perspective lies in the massive adoption of mobile shopping in 2020. Mobile e-commerce recorded an impressive 68 percent value growth in 2020, with a forecast for further growth at 30 percent overall value until 2025 (Dan, 2021d). Romania had been well positioned to witness such an increase in large part due to fast 4G mobile internet connections, which represent 61 percent of the total mobile internet in the country (Dan, 2021d).

Consumers in Romania can benefit from several mobile solutions, such as mobile cash withdrawals offered by major banks (Transilvania and ING), or Scan & Pay mobile applications introduced by Kaufland and Carrefour (the largest grocery retailers). With growing trust towards mobile payments, further introduction of innovations in this sector is likely to gain consumers' attention.

The 2020 surge in digital shopping in Romania is not only due to an increased frequency of online shopping. Consumers were also exposed to a broader range of product categories that could be purchased online, building bigger and more diverse baskets (Cristea, 2021). The food and beverages category witnessed the biggest growth of 115 percent, albeit from a very minor share of 4 percent at the beginning of 2020 (Cristea, 2021).

The year 2020 was one of spectacular evolution of e-commerce for Romania thanks to the overlapping power of two factors: building trust among new users and the growing baskets of a base of customers who were already familiar with digital shopping. With the forecasts showing stable growth in digital shopping, new shopping behaviors will only gain more traction in the coming years.

4.8 Russia

Russia is the twelfth largest e-commerce market globally. With 2020's value growth of 45 percent (Poletajevas, 2021a), it is the third country globally (behind India and Brazil) with the highest e-commerce sales growth (Abrams, 2021, p. 4). As in other CEE countries, the COVID-19 pandemic has propelled the development of e-commerce as consumers increasingly chose contactless shopping.

In an already dynamic e-commerce market, in 2020 Russian consumers could benefit from a range of innovative and personalized offers, assortment expansion, and improved distribution systems from e-retailers. The price attractiveness of online offerings was the key driver for the e-commerce surge in a market that still had relatively low purchasing power.

The limited disposable income of Russian shoppers and the unprecedented conditions of 2020 propelled the highest growth in essential categories, such as grocery and home care (Poletajevas, 2021a). However, lifestyle products such as fashion and home accessories also recorded double-digit growth, proving the overall growing readiness of shoppers to turn to e-commerce for a broad portfolio of products. The biggest Russian e-retailer and online marketplace, Wildberries.ru, remained the strongest player, with a 15 percent value share in 2020 (Poletajevas, 2021a). Although maintaining a focus on fashion items, the store has a broad portfolio spanning from electronics, toys, and homeware.

Two other e-retailers with very strong positions in Russia are Mvideo.ru and OZON.ru. Both e-retailers have similar profiles, focused mainly on electronics and media, but they each put a major effort into broadening their categories.

Just like other CEE countries at the beginning of the pandemic, Russian e-commerce struggled to meet the massive increase in demand and the unprecedented scale of new orders, especially in the grocery category, which led to major disruptions in supply chains and delivery solutions.

However, during the pandemic, Russian e-retailers ramped up delivery services and new pick-up points across the country. OZON.ru added an additional 2,000 pick-up points to their already existing 5,000, building strategic partnerships with bricks-and-mortar retailers (Poletajevas, 2021a). Similar tactics were implemented by Mvideo.ru and Wildberries.ru to extend pick-up services in 2020. E-commerce pick-up points are quite unique to Russia, since they offer additional services, such as additional try-on services on the spot.

Key e-retailers in Russia have nationally focused sales, giving little space for cross-border commerce for foreign players. Already in 2019, cross-border e-commerce recorded slower growth than in previous years, mainly due to the continued development of local players (Poletajevas, 2021a). Additionally, a 2019 ruling from the Council of the Eurasian Economic Commission reduced the threshold for duty-free imports of foreign goods. Consequently, purchasers of items worth above €500 must now pay a fee equal to 30 percent of the value of the goods.

Nevertheless, in 2020, cross-border commerce surged as Russians sought products that were in short supply in the country (Poletajevas, 2021a). Strong international players, such as the Chinese AliExpress launched a partnership with the Mail.ru group, which unlocked infrastructure for Russian consumers, such as opening new warehouses and next-day delivery services. Even though AliExpress is facing challenges amid the entrenched position of domestic players, the Chinese marketplace has a 29-million strong consumer base and is planning an initial public offering (IPO) in the coming years (Marrow, 2021).

AliExpress also invested heavily in mobile commerce during 2020, and was the first player to offer product recognition via mobile cameras. Wildberries.ru and OZON.ru enabled mobile product research by scanning barcodes on their respective mobile applications. The Russian market has become a dynamic source of e-commerce innovations, backed by considerable financial investments. For example, Lamoda launched an augmented reality app for fitting shoes, designed by the Belarussian start-up Wannaby (Poletajevas, 2021b).

Leading e-retailers also took measures to make mobile shopping more convenient and enjoyable, as mobile e-commerce recorded a 64 percent value growth in 2020 (Poletajevas, 2021b). This form of digital shopping was reinforced by increasing penetration of mobile internet in Russia and the increased adoption of smartphones by the older population.

Increasing mobile commerce adoption also supports a growing trust in cashless payments among Russian shoppers and the market has seen an increased number of near-field communication (NFC) payments and mobile wallets such as Apple Pay (Poletajevas, 2021b). Convenience and functionality are becoming key for Russian consumers and mobile app functionalities are predicted to be key drivers of scalable e-commerce development in the country.

4.9 Slovakia

Slovakia is one of the few countries in the CEE region that already had a well-established e-commerce penetration and infrastructure before the pandemic of 2020. In 2019, six out of ten online store visitors were making digital purchases and the market boasted low administration fees, which further facilitated e-commerce investments. The year 2020 brought a 31 percent retail value sales increase, reaching €1.8 billion (Milasevic, 2021c). The forecasted e-commerce retail value increase is projected to be 13 percent by 2025.

During the COVID-19 pandemic Slovakian consumers shopped across more product categories and benefited from popular free delivery and easy return policies. All e-commerce players and categories recorded double-digit growth in 2020, with groceries nearly doubling in value (Milasevic, 2021c). The biggest players, such as Internet Mall Slovakia (Mall.sk) and Alza.sk managed to extend their portfolios by adding new categories, such as home office and fitness accessories, to fight for bigger market shares. However, the Slovakian e-commerce market is highly fragmented. Mall.sk posts a value share of 5 percent while being the market sales leader (Milasevic, 2021c). The company owns 300 click-and-collect locations and has extended its offering into electronics and consumer appliances; however, its leading position is threatened by a growing number of specialist e-retailers, who drive further market fragmentation in Slovakia.

Alza.sk, a relatively big online player with 2 percent e-commerce retail value share, is the only e-retailer to sell its own branded products at competitive prices. Slovakian consumers' overall adoption and trust in e-commerce allows

Alza.sk to benefit from the power of their e-commerce brand and offer competitive products in the market, which might become a lasting trend in Slovakia.

E-commerce market fragmentation is also due to the growing popularity of cross-border e-commerce. Product unavailability or higher prices led shoppers to e-commerce stores from China, Czech Republic, and Germany (Milasevic, 2021c). Sales from AliExpress doubled in 2020, but forthcoming tax legislation on all delivery parcels is expected to slow the surge of cross-border e-commerce. However, in Slovakia parcels of a value lower than €22 will be exempt from tax, still making them price competitive against domestic players (Milasevic, 2021c).

Slovakian shoppers are increasingly choosing cashless payments and mobile wallets like Apple Pay and Google Pay, which were introduced in 2019 and 2018 respectively. In 2020, more e-retailers allowed for mobile wallet payments, which contributed to mobile e-commerce retail value sales rising by 62 percent in 2020 (Milasevic, 2021f). Growth of mobile e-commerce is forecasted to reach 25 percent by 2025, ahead of total e-commerce growth in Slovakia. In recent years the country has recorded an average income growth and increased consumer confidence, which resulted in stronger purchase power. This factor has a direct effect on the growing value of e-commerce baskets, with apparel, footwear, and consumer electronics as the leading categories, including in mobile e-commerce (Milasevic, 2021f).

Slovakian e-commerce players have not yet invested in dedicated mobile applications, instead placing a stronger focus on mobile-optimized desktop websites. Alza.sk is one of the few pure e-commerce players with a dedicated app, while Mall.sk enhanced their omnichannel features with a barcode scanner in their application. However, investments in mobile e-commerce and innovations are set to rise, especially in such a competitive and fragmented market as Slovakia. Cash payments are anticipated to decline further and mobile is considered to be the leading touchpoint to increase the consumer base (Milasevic, 2021f).

Slovakia maintains a rather uneven distribution of e-commerce facilities, with internet connectivity and delivery services being much better developed in urban areas. E-retailers tend to offer free delivery only within a limited radius, and mobile commerce is also unevenly spread across the country (Milasevic, 2021f). Still, the 2020 pandemic created a strong incentive for e-retailer growth and key investments in e-commerce infrastructure will likely take place in due time.

4.10 Ukraine

In 2020, Ukrainian e-commerce recorded an impressive 59 percent value growth with a strong lead from domestic e-retailer Uaprom, reaching a 16 percent value share. The market is forecasted to grow by 18 percent until 2025 (Khoruzhyy, 2021c). As in all analyzed CEE countries, this rise is due to the COVID-19 pandemic and subsequent lockdowns, which forced consumers to switch to online shopping. The Ukrainian government facilitated the transition to digital shopping by permitting online orders of medical products and pharmaceuticals.

Numerous logistical solutions have recently been launched in Ukraine, which have facilitated e-commerce adoption in the country. Nearly 1,000 self-service pick-up points were launched by the Nova Poshta delivery service by the end of 2020 and Ukrposhta (the country's national postal carrier) partnered with SMART Forwarding to simplify cross-border sales from UK-based e-retailers (Khoruzhyy, 2021c). Major Polish fashion retailers belonging to LPP Holding opened their online platforms, following in the steps of the global giant Inditex, which has successfully operated in Ukraine since 2019.

The e-commerce surge led to more market fragmentation and third-party merchants became a significant force on the market, with a 13 percent value share. The leading categories for Ukrainian shoppers are consumer electronics and fashion, though grocery shopping recorded considerable growth during the pandemic.

Despite growing value and penetration, Ukrainian e-commerce is struggling to evolve in terms of payment methods. Shoppers have low trust in online payment methods and cash-on-delivery is by far the most common choice (Khoruzhyy, 2021c). E-retailers are currently offering dedicated incentives and promotions for online payments and mobile wallets are heavily advertised. Indeed, mobile e-commerce might be the biggest facilitator of online payments, since its value share grew by 83 percent in 2020 (Khoruzhyy, 2021f).

Interestingly, mobile commerce in Ukraine has been driven by two major sectors – food delivery (Zakaz.ua, Glovo, and Raketa) and cross-border commerce (AliExpress). AliExpress has been among the first to incentivize online purchases and cashless payments within the app with discounts (Khoruzhyy, 2021c). The Chinese e-retail giant has successfully taken over the mobile commerce market, with free delivery for all purchases. Further investments in e-commerce from domestic players will need to be put in place to maintain the e-commerce growth from local players.

4.11 CEE E-Commerce Market Overview

Even though the analyzed CEE countries show differences in terms of digital market development, the consumer-led digital shift makes the speed of regional digitization almost on par with the largest European countries (Ignatowicz, 2018, p. 44). However, significant market-level discrepancies shed light on the uneven journey which must be undertaken by governments and businesses to develop the regional e-commerce sector.

Analysis of year-on-year retailing sales value of e-commerce shows the very strong position of Russia. The country boasts the steepest forecasted e-commerce growth curve until 2025 in terms of retail selling price value. Being the twelfth largest e-commerce market globally with a population of 144 million, it is by far the strongest player among other CEE markets. The second strongest player in the region, in terms of sales value, is Poland (Figure 1).

By omitting Russia and Poland from the e-commerce sales analysis, it can be observed that the Czech Republic, Romania, and Ukraine are next in line in terms of the level of current retail sales volume and forecasted growth (Figure 2). Hungary, Slovakia, Belarus, and Bulgaria are forecasted to remain relatively smaller markets in terms of e-commerce sales.

In terms of total e-commerce growth between 2019 and 2020, the steepest rise, of about 50 percent, can be observed in Ukraine and Bulgaria, largely induced by the COVID-19 pandemic, although all countries recorded unprecedented, double-digit growth (Figure 3).

All the analyzed CEE markets show a differentiated e-retailer structure. The top three e-retailers represent between 25 and 45 percent of the total market shares. E-commerce markets are concentrated in Belarus, Poland, Ukraine, and

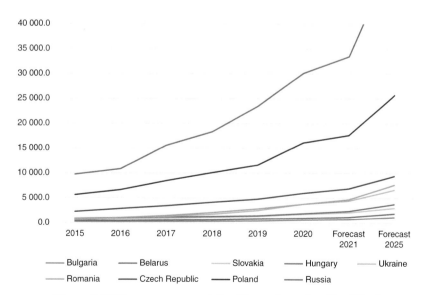

Figure 1 CEE e-commerce retail selling price value (€ million)
Source: Authors' own study based on diverse Euromonitor data from trade sources and national statistics (2021).

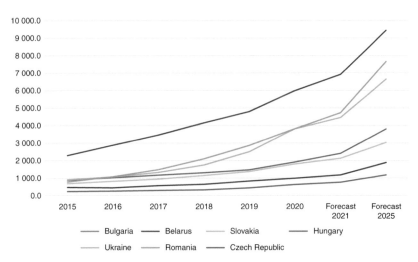

Figure 2 CEE e-commerce retail selling price value (€ million) excluding Russia and Poland

Source: Authors' own study based on diverse Euromonitor data from trade sources and national statistics (2021).

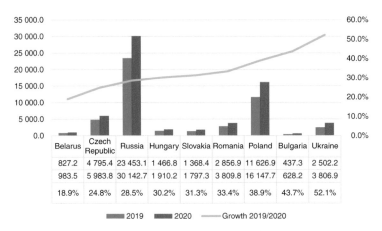

Figure 3 Total CEE e-commerce growth 2019/2020

Source: Authors' own study based on diverse Euromonitor data from trade sources and national statistics (2021).

Romania, with the top three players accounting for over 35 percent of the market (Figure 4).

In most cases, the top players have their shares spread relatively evenly. Poland has a unique set-up in this comparison, with the Allegro marketplace taking as much as 33 percent of the total e-commerce market shares. Belarus, Ukraine, and Romania also display strong leadership from their top three

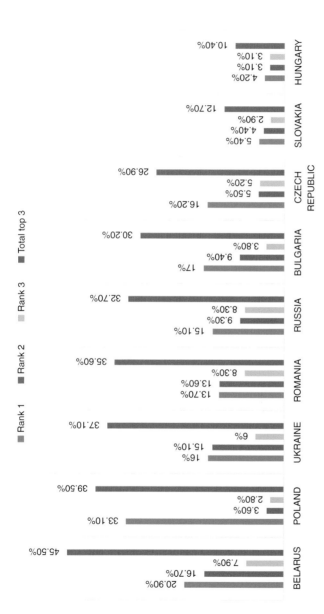

Figure 4 Top three 2020 e-commerce shares per market

Source: Authors' own study based on diverse Euromonitor data from trade sources and national statistics (2021).

players, leaving little space for competition in the respective markets. In contrast, Slovakia and Hungary remain highly fragmented, with the biggest players only accounting for up to 5 percent of the total market (Figure 5).

The presentation of the top players offers a significant insight into how the power is spread among the biggest e-retailers and what the preferences of consumers are. The massive shifts of 2020 unlocked a host of opportunities for e-retailers, who aim to leverage the new and lasting trends across the region.

5 Key E-Commerce Trends in CEE

Even though CEE markets are diversified in terms of market volumes and digitization levels, there are some patterns that span across the markets. E-commerce in the region has been evolving with the strengthening power of marketplaces and cross-border players. Consumers in CEE showed relatively similar reactions to the unprecedented conditions of the 2020 pandemic, which propelled the rise of new categories in e-commerce and a surge in m-commerce. A deep dive into these changes sheds light onto the possible future developments in the region.

5.1 The Power of Marketplaces

Across Europe, the biggest e-commerce players come from the West, which dominates the European e-commerce industry. Among the biggest e-commerce companies, the top five are from Germany, France, and the United Kingdom (*Top 100 E-Commerce Retailers in Europe*, 2020). However, in terms of monthly visits, the Polish e-commerce marketplace Allegro has entered the top-ten list of the biggest e-commerce websites in the world. The website welcomes almost 194 million visitors per month and is the only player on the top-ten list that operates exclusively in Europe (*Allegro Enters Top 10 Biggest E-Commerce Websites*, 2020).

Allegro was launched in 1999 and has had a significant impact on the entire Polish digital landscape. It started as an auction platform for niche products among hobbyists. Although it still remains an auction platform, this role has been overshadowed by its operations as a marketplace with fixed-price products and a variety of services for customers and sellers. Interestingly, Allegro operates on individual product cards, unlike Amazon, where one product page can be used by multiple sellers. This difference, although laborious for sellers who need to prepare descriptions for every product independently, helps build transparent offerings and a stronger presence of sellers on the platform.

The power of marketplaces can be observed across the entire CEE region. These online platforms provide infrastructure to smaller players, who are at the

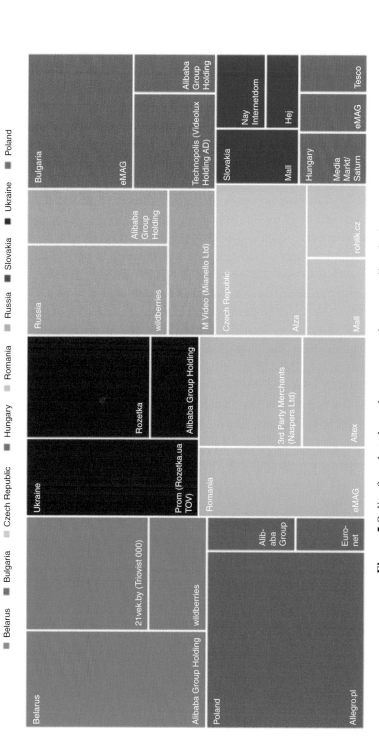

Figure 5 Split of market shares between top three e-retailers in CEE

Source: Authors' own study based on diverse Euromonitor data from trade sources and national statistics (2021).

frontline of any nascent digital economy. However, amid the e-commerce surge, marketplaces also attract bigger players, combining scale, price competitiveness, and a broad product selection on one website. Amazon, the biggest marketplace in the world, is proof of how successful such models can be.

In CEE, marketplaces are the leading e-commerce platforms, enjoying double-digit market share among the top-ten players in every analyzed country (Figure 6). The top performers in every country show a consistent spread of shares among leading marketplaces (global or local) and category-based shop formats.

Notably, local marketplaces have a strong position in CEE, which proves the high functionality of the format in the region. Apart from Polish Allegro, another notable marketplace is eMAG – the largest e-commerce platform in Romania, with over half a million unique customers every day. Sellers can list their products in over 1,600 product categories, the most popular being car accessories, home appliances, children's toys, sport, and fashion. eMag. ro is also one of the four European e-commerce marketplaces that established International Marketplace Network (IMN) in 2019 – a platform through which sellers gain access to a joint market of 230 million potential customers (Constantin, 2019). IMN offers an interface that enables sellers to use a single point of work and synchronize their offerings on each of the four platforms. The Network is also beneficial for shoppers, by driving cross-border competitiveness and bigger selection of goods. As Emmanuel Grenier, CEO of Cdiscount (one of IMN's members) has claimed: "it is an important achievement at European level, which underlines the dynamic and

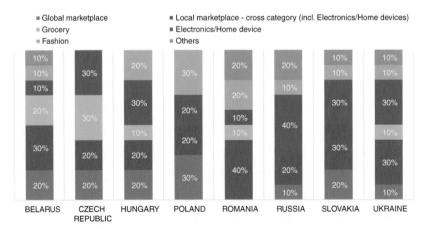

Figure 6 Top-ten e-commerce players – 2020 market shares by category
Source: Authors' own study based on diverse Euromonitor data from trade sources and national statistics (2021).

innovative character of marketplace-type online trading networks" (Constantin, 2019).

The growing popularity of digital marketplaces can be attributed to the lasting power of key consumer trends. Consumers are constantly seeking convenience and price-competitiveness in online shopping. Multibrand e-retailers match their expectations with a vast array of goods, available in one place, and with facilitated price comparison features. The competitive pressure of marketplaces caters to shoppers' needs. Furthermore, Millennials and Gen Z have growing expectations towards online shopping that fuel personalization and a more niche approach towards business set-up (Power, 2021). Businesses in the United States are beginning to open up to more specialized and niche marketplaces, which might be an interesting future opportunity for digital-savvy shoppers around the globe, including in CEE.

With growing consumer interest, marketplaces start to attract not only more shoppers, but also more sellers. Marketplaces rely on them to provide a differentiated value proposition that is not just driven by price; however, they still miss out on sufficient seller-support options. Even though digital marketplaces have gained traction over the last decade, many brands and businesses are still reluctant to enter them, due to aggressive competition, lack of cooperation between marketplaces and sellers, and limited control over sales and data. Briedis et al. (2020) outline a set of best practices to look for in a successful marketplace:

- facilitated transactions among multiple sellers and customers – business model should allow easy access either to B2C (business-to-consumer) or C2C (consumer-to-consumer) sellers and allow for a stand-alone marketplace format or a combination of retail and marketplace (i.e. Amazon)
- access to multiple brands – offerings can focus on a specific product group, a category, or a diverse product portfolio
- transparent fee structures – assisting sellers that pay referral fees to gain access to consumer base and detailed data points
- additional fee-based services that enable order fulfillment, such as warehousing, last-mile delivery, return policy, customer service management, and payment processing
- services to seller's consumer network, such as search support, data processing and analytics
- quality management assistance and product authentication support (Briedis, Choi, Huang, and Kohli, 2021).

With consumers' growing trust and continuous growth of marketplaces in CEE, businesses should investigate building or strengthening their operations on these platforms. Both traditional and digital-only brands can benefit from a presence on marketplaces, "however additional measures need to be taken to secure business effectiveness, since participation in a marketplace means adding a channel that cannot be managed as other wholesale and direct-to-consumer (DTC) channels are" (Briedis, Choi, Huang, and Kohli, 2021). Sellers do not retain full control over product pricing, making it difficult to forecast revenue and avoid on-platform price competition. The marketing strategy is also dictated by the capabilities of the marketplace, which might affect a brand's narrative. Therefore, brands concerned about their perception and tone should negotiate specific conditions that would facilitate on-site consumer experience and branding consistency across platforms.

Defining a winning marketplace approach requires strategic planning that will leverage the benefits of a massive consumer base without the risks that the format brings to unprepared sellers.

5.2 Emerging Product Categories – Fashion and Grocery

The growth of e-commerce platforms has also been dictated by product categories. In 2017, the penetration of online sales in CEE markets was focused mainly on media (books, music, and video), computer software, and consumer electronics. Fashion and apparel, footwear, and home furnishings were considered niche, while beauty and grocery categories barely existed online (Namysł, Jurkanis, Yearwood, and Sikora, 2019, p. 5). In terms of building category diversity across e-commerce portfolios, the significance of the 2020 surge cannot be underrated. Even though e-commerce had already been considered the largest growth driver for multiple categories, including fashion and grocery back in 2017, no projection included the jump that occurred in CEE in 2020.

The fashion category has had a record growth in the region since 2020. Bulgaria, Moldova, and Russia were the key markets where online fashion sales accounted for a significant share of total online sales, but this sector has shown a significant increase in all the analyzed markets. Interestingly, pure online players continue to dominate the fashion and apparel sector. Even though brand.com players and bricks-and-mortar retailers also benefited from the shift to e-commerce, they have been unable to achieve market shares that could compete with the leading pure players in the respective markets. German BonPrix is one of the key fashion pure players in Slovakia, Ukraine, Hungary, and the Czech Republic, whilst Zalando and About You have strong positions in the Czech Republic, Hungary, Poland, Romania, and Slovakia (*Top Sites Ranking for Lifestyle and Fashion Apparel*, 2021).

BonPrix belongs to the German Otto Group and operates in over 30 countries as one of online fashion's global leaders. The brand was launched in 1986 as a mail-order company specializing in apparel and opened its online store in 1997. Nowadays the company caters for over 35 million consumers annually by successfully merging physical retail, e-commerce, and catalogue selling (Stratten, 2020). BonPrix mainly sells its five private-label brands of women's, men's, and children's fashion, as well as home textiles, and interior design accessories. Monthly changes to its product portfolio and a value-for-money pricing policy have allowed the company to build a strong and broad target audience for their offering.

Currently as much as 85 percent of Bon Prix's revenue comes from e-commerce, and over 50 percent of the revenue is generated outside Germany. The company invests heavily in building an omnichannel strategy with physical shopping experiences. Showrooms are designed to showcase products, but also connect customers to the BonPrix digital platform with digital screens and interactive product presentations. Additionally, the BonPrix mobile application works in-store as a personal shopping assistant as well as a remote control during the visit. The check-out is also optimized with an integrated in-app purchase option, allowing the customers to avoid queues and shop directly from the fitting rooms.

Although omnichannel experience is considered a major trend for the fashion industry, Zalando – a digital pure player – is considered one of Europe's biggest success stories. The company was founded in Germany in 2009 and launched an aggressive multimarket expansion. Zalando currently operates in 17 markets as an online fashion and beauty platform (Ribeiro, 2020). The Zalando website records around 260 million monthly visits, with around 79 percent of them through its mobile application (Ribeiro, 2020). The company's product portfolio covers over 2,500 brands, ranging from value-for-money to luxury items. Its main competitive advantage lies in generous shipping and return policies, which have set the standard for other online fashion retailers globally. Logistics for the CEE region are facilitated through Zalando's first international fulfillment center, opened in Poland. Zalando has also started to develop an offline strategy, with physical store openings around key European locations. Namysł et al. (2019) call the approach a "digital land grab," which means expansion of fashion e-commerce players into previously uncharted territories (Namysł, Jurkanis, Yearwood, and Sikora, 2019, p. 6). From physical stores to independent fulfillment centers, large e-commerce players are aggressively building up their product and business portfolio.

Russia is the only country in CEE where the leading position in the fashion category is taken by a local e-retailer, Lamoda. The platform was launched in

2010 by Niels Tonsen, who had previously worked on the Zalando project in the German incubator Rocket Internet. In 2013 Lamoda received a €130 million investment from JP Morgan – the biggest injection in the history of Russian e-retailers.

Lamoda.ru dynamically expanded from footwear retail to fashion and home accessories, effectively taking over the sector as the number-one go-to fashion e-commerce store in Russia. There is a visible similarity between Lamoda and other Western-based fashion e-retailers like Zalando. Its rapid success is due to major investments in fulfillment and delivery solutions – an essential element for fashion e-commerce, especially in a market where postal services remain unreliable, and consumers prefer to pay cash upon delivery (Lunden, 2013). Namysł et al. state that "the time lag between discovery and purchase is a pain-point for customers who continue to expect better experiences" (Namysł, Jurkanis, Yearwood, and Sikora, 2019, p. 6). A focus on reducing this friction is a building block to consumer loyalty. A self-managed delivery network, Lamoda Express, offers next-day delivery and try-on services in multiple cities across Russia. The try-on services secure customer experience but also drive cost-efficiency via limited returns. Just like Zalando, delivery policies are Lamoda's competitive edge – free shipping and fast delivery create a convenient shopping experience and help to win consumer trust.

In 2019 Lamoda developed a marketplace model, involving over 2,000 partners (*Lamoda posts 23.5% sales growth year-on-year*, 2019). The portfolio was also expanded to jewelry and beauty and personal care products. Lamoda also operates in Belarus, Ukraine, and Kazakhstan, where it is gradually gaining market shares. Going forward, brands in CEE might face the challenge either to invest heavily in their own online sales channels or join the growing power of online pure play multi-brand e-retailers and marketplaces.

Grocery, a category that barely existed in CEE e-commerce before the COVID-19 pandemic, recorded at least double-digit growth in almost every country in the region in 2020. Grocery shopping acceleration in Europe had been projected for almost a decade, but the market has been slow to adapt. Galante et al. stated in 2013 that while consumers might be ready to choose a more convenient way of grocery shopping, e-retailers had not yet secured reliable solutions to provide a frictionless shopping experience for fresh produce (Galante, Garcia-Lopez, and Monroe, 2013, p. 23). With poor supply, grocery e-commerce suffered from low demand and this stagnating pattern had remained in CEE until the COVID-19 pandemic, when shoppers were forced to limit offline shopping and turn to digital alternatives. Consumer skepticism about product quality, which had hitherto dominated popular opinion about online food shopping (Galante, Garcia-Lopez, and Monroe, 2013, p. 23) was overturned amid the lockdowns, with thousands of consumers eventually shopping for fresh produce online, many of whom were doing so for the first time.

In Europe overall, grocery e-commerce recorded growth of around 55 percent in 2020, in comparison with an average gain of 10 percent in 2019 (Verscheueren et al., 2021, p. 10). Average offline growth rates were relatively modest at that time – between 3 and 12 percent in hypermarkets, supermarkets, and discounters. What is more, online channels contributed to an astonishing 20 percent of total grocery revenue growth in 2020, despite having a modest 4 percent market share in 2019 (Verscheueren et al., 2021, p. 10). In Western Europe, especially in countries such as the United Kingdom, with an already recognizable online grocery penetration, the biggest players captured significant market shares. In nascent e-grocery markets, such as those of CEE, multiple new players managed to successfully establish their presence.

The impressive growth of 2020 for e-grocery might even be underrepresenting the overall market potential, given how many players were unable to keep up with the sudden surge in demand. At the onset of the pandemic, several larger grocery retailers experienced major capacity and distribution constraints that compromised customer satisfaction (Tjon Pian Gi and Spielvogel, 2021). One of the biggest Polish grocery e-retailers, Frisco.pl, was forced to extend delivery times to up to one month. E-retailers were not ready for the logistical challenges, as their distribution centers were not ready to stock up and fulfill the orders. The backend e-commerce processes were also overwhelmed, causing prolonged website loading times and application crashes. E-retailers looked for innovative solutions to solve these unprecedented issues by optimizing e-commerce processes and pushing for digital innovations on their platforms.

Verscheueren et al. claim that shopping frictions during the first months of mass e-grocery shopping might have caused demand shifts, leaving many consumers frustrated with their experiences (Verscheueren et al., 2021, p. 13). However, initial research shows that consumers are likely to continue with their shopping habits after COVID-19 and their spending intent for e-grocery might drop by just 10 percent (Verscheueren et al., 2021, p. 13). Moreover, the more often consumers bought groceries online in 2020, the more likely they are to increase their share of online buying in years to come (Verscheueren et al., 2021, p. 25).

Consumers appreciated the newfound convenience of shopping online for food as smaller and more agile players took hold of the opportunity by offering instant mobile shopping delivery from nearby offline stores and managed to shape a new shopping experience. The initial frictions caused by exponential demand growth brought major platform innovations and improvements in supply chains.

Although grocery players in CEE are still in their early stages and have not yet managed to achieve strong market shares, the success of services like Glovo in Ukraine and e-dostavka in Belarus prove the growing consumer adaptation to e-grocery solutions.

Glovo is a Spanish on-demand delivery platform, which has recently announced further expansion into CEE (*Glovo Announces Multiple Acquisitions ...,* 2021). In a series of acquisition deals the company is taking over Delivery Hero, one of the world's leading local delivery platforms. This way, Glovo's footprint will expand into Bosnia Herzegovina, Bulgaria, Croatia, Montenegro, Romania, and Serbia. The aggressive go-to-market strategy is based on the company's forecast that CEE consumers have embraced on-demand delivery platforms, especially in the e-grocery sector. Glovo secured a €450 million investment round in early 2021, which will be dedicated to international expansion and technological development. Glovo's focus is Q-commerce (quick-commerce), which means ultra-fast, almost instantaneous delivery of small quantities of goods to customers. Q-commerce is targeted at users that need a particular set of items delivered quickly, which is the opposite of routine-based bulk-shopping.

The development of Q-commerce is possible with a broad network of delivery couriers and so-called dark stores, which are located across strategic locations and offer the most popular and most shopped products. As well as dark stores, Glovo builds relationships with hyper- and supermarkets, such as Carrefour, Tesco, and Kaufland, and develops its own infrastructure and fulfillment centers.

The Czech-based online grocery retailer Rohlik also proves that there is growing potential in the e-grocery sector. A distinctive business model of the startup puts it midway between a quick delivery service and an online supermarket. The Rohlik Group secured an impressive €100 million investment in July 2021 and is valued at €1 billion (Van Rompaey, 2021). The company is using the pandemic-induced momentum to expand into other European markets, including Germany, Romania, Italy, France, and Spain. The company also operates in Hungary under the brand Kifli.hu. The Rohlik Group is focusing on the mobile grocery shopping trend and consumers' need for fast delivery. Shoppers are offered an array of 17,000 products and groceries, which are sourced from wholesale items, goods from partners (i.e., Marks & Spencer) and products from local sellers. Diversification of product sourcing allows the company to adapt the portfolio to market demand and personalize the offering to consumer needs. Rohlik is being praised for its unique business model that aims to bring growth to small businesses, which are usually the first to suffer due to the expansion of big online players. The inclusion of local businesses allows the company to build a more attractive and competitive product offering, which can stand out among the overly similar offers from other grocers. Most importantly, all the products can be delivered within two hours.

The typical e-grocery consumer is focused on weekly grocery shopping, not impulse purchases of small-value products. This behavior pattern increases the average basket value to €60–100 (Van Rompaey, 2021). This approach allows the company to grow and avoid losses caused by the delivery costs of low-value shopping.

COVID-19-induced changes in consumer demand will shape the grocery retail market, and Gerckens et al. (2021) outline five key shifts in the sector:

1. online becomes core
2. value-for-money products are gaining importance
3. consumers expect higher quality at entry-level price tiers
4. brick-and-mortar supermarkets are losing share
5. consumer lifestyle agendas drive demand through focus on health, sustainability, and convenience food.

More than 60 percent of European consumers changed their shopping behaviors during the pandemic and the biggest shift can be observed with regards to consumer loyalty, with 30 percent of shoppers changing their stores (Verscheueren et al., 2021, p. 13). Shoppers switched to outlets that offered better value for money and convenience, such as easy access and delivery options. These behaviors open opportunities for online grocery as digital solutions can fit perfectly to these changing consumer needs. Importantly, even if CEE shoppers have a lower disposable income than Western Europeans, research shows that the shift towards e-grocery will continue throughout all income segments, with lower-income consumers possibly moving towards e-commerce solutions that offer value-for-money products and competitive pricing (Gerckens et al., 2021). A continued polarization of consumers is projected, "with lower-income consumers expecting to focus more on saving money and overall downtrading, while higher-income segments' product preferences may drive them to overall upgrading despite increasing price sensitivity" (Gerckens et al., 2021).

Gerckens et al. (2021) observe that one of the biggest challenges for e-grocery lies in building awareness and trust among new users. Only 7 percent of consumers who did not shop for groceries online in 2020 show any intention of buying online in 2021 (Verscheueren et al., 2021, p. 26). E-grocery players will need to build competitive offerings and trust among new consumer bases.

Throughout the turbulent year 2020, consumers switched their habits, which positively impacted upon the development of e-grocery. The keys to continued business growth are investment and setting clear key performance indicators (KPIs) for the sector, such as optimization of marketing mix, raising e-commerce awareness through business units, and online-specific strategies and frameworks (Caccia, 2020). Due to the novelty of e-grocery, businesses might be tempted to gradually lose focus on the budding e-commerce opportunity. What is more, consumers might still switch their needs, develop new shopping barriers, and build demand for new types of e-grocery solutions. Businesses need to build a flexible approach towards innovation and development, since creating a consumer-driven strategy will be the key to compete in the e-grocery sector.

5.3 Cross-Border Players

It is significant that the top performers in the fashion and grocery category are mostly foreign players. Cross-border e-commerce has developed strongly over the past years, especially in the fashion category, but also because of the major entry of the Chinese pure player AliExpress in most CEE markets. AliExpress is a subsidiary of Alibaba Ltd., a Chinese integrated retail platform, combining data and technology services (AliCloud), logistics (Cainiao), and payment tools (Alipay). The company's long-term goal is global expansion of an international e-commerce marketplace, combining the Chinese Alibaba portal and AliExpress – a marketplace built in 2010 to service cross-border e-commerce (Hu, 2021, p. 3). In 2020 Alibaba Ltd. held second place (behind Walmart) in global retailing and boasts the highest projected CAGR growth (11 percent) among all the top-ten global retailers (Hu, 2021, p. 5). E-commerce remains Alibaba's main source of revenue, leading in China with 12 percent of the market share. However, thanks to its aggressive cross-border policy, Russia was Alibaba's third top country in terms of sales volume (behind China and Turkey) in 2020. AliExpress is currently localized for buyers all over the world, with translations in 18 languages. The platform no longer sells products only from Chinese merchants and has since expanded to enable local sellers to use the portal in their own markets. Interestingly, Alibaba's go-to-market strategy usually involves acquisition of major local e-commerce players, like the Turkish Trendyol or the Singapore-based Lazada, which is the leading e-commerce platform in Indonesia, Malaysia, the Philippines, Singapore, Thailand, and Vietnam. These acquisitions allow Alibaba to rapidly build a presence in a foreign market. Entering Alibaba's orbit might be attractive to merchants and e-retailers, who benefit from network effect and significant investments. One of the most important benefits for CEE markets is the possibility to facilitate distribution and ease the logistics burden, which in 2020 proved to be a major disruption to many CEE players. Cainiao (an Alibaba Ltd. logistics subsidiary) opened a new international air-freight route in 2020 to speed up delivery times between China and Europe by over 30 percent (Hu, 2021, p. 20). This way, cross-border parcels from China can be delivered within ten days, or sooner if the items are stored in one of Alibaba's overseas warehouses.

According to Hu (2021), Russia is the only CEE market considered a priority in Alibaba's cross-border strategy. However a country deep-dive shows big consumer interest in AliExpress' offering due to its broad product selection and competitive prices. Belarus, Ukraine, and Slovakia are among the countries where AliExpress disrupted local e-commerce the most. However tax legislation on cross-border deliveries is expected to slow the surge of cross-border e-commerce.

Across the entire CEE region, it can be observed that AliExpress is the most powerful cross-border player. It is listed among the top-ten e-commerce stores in the eight analyzed countries (Table 1). No other e-retailer can boast such coverage; eMAG is second and enjoys a strong position in three of the analyzed countries. eMAG was founded in 2001 in Romania and later expanded into Bulgaria and Hungary. In 2012 the South Africa-based Naspers media group acquired a 70 percent stake in eMAG and propelled technological development of the platform and new subsidiaries. In early 2021, eMAG announced prioritized investments in regional expansion, technology development, and logistics (Banila, 2021). Currently the eMAG group comprises of not only one e-retailer platform, but also the online stores Fashion Days, PC Garage, a courier company, repair shop, online marketing agency, home delivery platform, and a software company. The company also plans expansion into another international market (the specifics had not been revealed while preparing this Element) and to strengthen marketplace operations (Chirileasa, 2021). eMAG also continues to develop its omnichannel operations by opening showrooms in strategic locations. Offline showrooms in Hungary and Bulgaria take premium locations and showcase a broad array of electronics, home appliances, personal care products, toys, and accessories.

Cross-border e-commerce is more popular among shoppers from developed economies (Cheliński and Szymkowiak, 2021, p. 5). High delivery costs, extended delivery times, and a lack of website translations are key blockers for cross-border shopping. However, players like Alibaba or Amazon are successfully addressing these barriers. Continuous expansion of international e-retailers into developing markets is building new consumer bases in

Table 1 Cross-border e-retailers across CEE markets

E-Retailer	Belarus	Bulgaria	Czech Republic	Hungary	Romania	Russia	Slovakia	Ukraine	Poland	Total
Aliexpress	1	1	1	1		1	1	1	1	8
Emag		1		1	1					3
Lamoda	1					1				2
Alza			1				1			2
Wildberries	1					1				2
Tesco			1	1						2
Mall			1				1			2
Amazon.com	1						1			2

Source: Authors' own study based on diverse Euromonitor data from trade sources and national statistics (2021).

developing countries. Research by the Polish Chamber of Electronic Economy revealed that Polish consumers are eager to shop cross-border due to lower prices and increasingly attractive delivery options (Cheliński and Szymkowiak, 2021, p. 9). The most shopped categories are fashion and electronics, which tallies with consumers in more developed economies.

Central and Eastern Europe can benefit from the presence of cross-border players, who offer access to e-commerce solutions in countries that have not yet developed sufficient local structures and businesses for online shopping. Nevertheless, the innovation and convenience brought to consumers by international e-commerce giants, especially in mobile commerce, might allow foreign players such as AliExpress to take over burgeoning digital economies, such as Bulgaria and Belarus.

The COVID-19 pandemic has drastically impacted upon the private business of small and medium-sized enterprises (SMEs), that is, companies with fewer than 250 employees. Importantly, SMEs are the backbone of the CEE economy, since 99 percent of businesses in the region are SMEs and they account for two-thirds of all jobs (Iszkowska et al., 2021, p. 38).

The SME companies were vulnerable to the impact of the pandemic due to cashflow problems and limited capability to sustain supply chains. Before the pandemic, 80 percent of SMEs in the CEE region had a website, but only 27 percent of them had a shopping function (Iszkowska et al., 2021, p. 39). It should be noted that this proportion is no different from other European countries. The gap occurs however in the level of spending on digital advertising, including social media. Markets in CEE spent between 9 and 12 percent less on online marketing (Iszkowska et al., 2021, p. 38).

In e-commerce especially, factors such as liquidity, supply chain, and advertising budgets put a major strain on local players. In return, they open the market to bigger international players, which might be less affected by supply and liquidity issues and might have bigger marketing budgets at their disposal. However, even the rise of SME cross-border e-commerce players was visible in 2020 in CEE countries, accounting for 8 percent of the total online sales (Iszkowska et al., 2021, p. 39).

5.4 Mobile E-Commerce Surge

Retail sales via mobile devices are rising faster than overall e-commerce sales, both globally and in the CEE region and this pattern is forecasted to remain until 2025, although the gap between annual growth rates will shrink (Abrams, 2021, p. 7). Central and Eastern Europe was second globally (behind Latin America) in terms of retail mobile commerce sales growth, with an average of 28 percent

(Abrams, 2021, p. 10). The markets of CEE are forecasted to record very significant growth until 2025, especially in the Czech Republic, Russia, and Slovakia) (Figure 7).

The countries of CEE are well developed in terms of mobile broadband coverage of above 99 percent. In 2019 Slovakia had the lowest Long-Term Evolution (LTE) availability at 98.4 percent of households covered. Romania recorded the highest LTE coverage increase (above 2 percentage points) (*Broadband Coverage in Europe*, 2019, p. 38). However, Iszkowska et al. (2021) observe that the CEE region may face further challenges regarding 5G deployment (Iszkowska et al., 2021, p. 24). With 92 percent of global operators planning the launch of ultra-fast broadband by 2022, CEE might lag with measures to introduce the technology. Even though EU countries are obliged to introduce 5G in at least one city in 2021, the cost of the operations is almost four times higher compared to the previous 4G technology (Iszkowska et al., 2021, p. 24). With 5G, users can benefit from up to 100 times higher connection speed, practically eliminating latency and allowing faster adoption of Internet of Things and Artificial Intelligence. 5G could lead to massive improvements in efficiency and convenience of mobile data usage, however CEE consumers might wait much longer for the mass introduction of the technology and then be reluctant to switch in case operators push their operating costs onto customers. Currently CEE countries are expected to reach only 19 percent 5G penetration by 2024, less than half the level of Western Europe (Iszkowska et al., 2021, p. 24).

The surge of mobile e-commerce (m-commerce) has been attributed to consumers' changing, busy lifestyles and is an answer to shoppers' growing

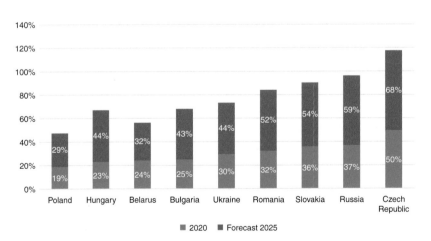

Figure 7 Share of mobile sales in total e-commerce in CEE
Source: Authors' own study based on diverse Euromonitor data from trade sources and national statistics (2021).

mobility. Mobile usage grows exponentially (Booth, 2020). As much as lifestyle has propelled the surge of mobile technologies, 2020 proved that even with dramatically decreased mobility (due to lockdowns), smartphones were often the device of choice for product research and shopping. The preference to purchase products online grew globally. In Europe, 39 percent of purchases took place via mobile devices and 48 percent via desktop (Mander, Buckle, and Hopkins, 2021, p. 20). The split is even more obvious from a generational perspective. Globally, half of baby boomers (aged 57–64) shopped via desktop (PC or laptop), compared to only 27 percent of Generation Z (aged 16–23) (Mander, Buckle, and Hopkins, 2021, p. 20).

A surge in mobile e-commerce was visible across all the analyzed CEE states in 2020. As e-retailers and bricks-and-mortar stores sought to rapidly grow their consumer base during ensuing lockdowns, mobile applications, and mobile-optimized websites turned out to be an efficient driver of traffic and transactions. However, consumer demand was not the only motivation for increased mobile focus. In 2019, Google, the biggest web browser in the world, launched mobile-first indexing for all new domains. This update meant prioritization in search results for websites with mobile-optimized pages over those which were not adapted to mobile devices. Since a vast majority of clicks on Google take place on the top three links on the results page, search ranking is a top priority to all online businesses. Website readiness for mobile screens is therefore a must for e-retail, both from a consumer and search algorithm perspective.

Lack of mobile interface for e-commerce websites is a challenge for many CEE e-retailers. Since mobile shopping only surged in 2020 in a majority of the markets, mobile-ready optimization had previously been deprioritized, especially in Slovakia (Milasevic, 2021f). Another challenge is mobile applications' availability exclusively for Android or iOS mobile-operating systems. With ongoing multi-dimensional development of mobile strategies, e-retailers should build a more consumer-friendly ecosystem that will be able to facilitate mobile commerce.

Continuous improvement of the m-commerce environment should be at the core of e-retailers' strategies. Online pure players have the potential to be at the forefront of mobile transformation, due to their sharp focus on a single, online channel. Multichannel players need to balance operations across online and offline touchpoints, which may lead to reprioritization of digital and mobile solutions, because of smaller revenue and lower reach. Nevertheless, consumer adoption of mobile technologies is forecasted to advance steadily between 2021 and 2025. Use of mobile phones, not only for shopping, but for product discovery and comparison, leads to an increasing need to create relevant, convenient solutions adapted for mobile devices.

The case of the Czech Republic shows how mobile-first innovation can encourage consumers to purchases on their smartphones. In the early years of mobile e-commerce in the country, mobile devices were used primarily for initial product research. Purchases and payments were made on desktop devices due to poor mobile web design and a scarcity of mobile applications. With continuous growth of internet connectivity, mobile optimization, and the evolution of mobile wallets, the last phases of purchase were also kept within the mobile environment (Milasevic, 2021b).

The mobile payments industry is reshaping how consumers perceive convenience online. In a majority of analyzed CEE markets cash-on-delivery is still one of the most preferred payment methods, but with m-commerce growth, consumers have leap-frogged to mobile payments relatively easily. During the COVID-19 pandemic consumers embraced contactless payment methods and adapted their shopping habits to a range of cashless payments. Retailers also opened up to new methods, unlocking either global opportunities, like Apple Pay and Google Pay, or local solutions. Vendors sought to develop trustworthy payment methods in local CEE markets that encouraged shoppers to switch to cashless payments. Tokenized bank cards, particularly popular in Hungary, are a relevant example of trust-building innovation. Tokens protect personal and other sensitive data by replacing it with an algorithmically generated number. This data is stored in the mobile application, similarly to virtual cards (Dan, 2021b).

Consumers are ready for m-commerce but only once a convenient and trustworthy environment has been created by retailers. Therefore, the improvement of mobile services will become increasingly important for those e-retailers who aim to scale up and build digital ecosystems relevant to shoppers' needs.

Conclusions

Strong e-commerce and mobile e-commerce are key factors that can help build a strong digital economy. The CEE region faces major opportunities but also challenges in terms of overall digitization and digital shopping. Negative macro-trends are taking place in the region, such as declining birthrates, emigration, and aging populations. Alongside growing demand for technological skills, the region could find itself stagnating, with an insufficient workforce of technological experts, who are essential for driving innovation.

The consumer behaviors of CEE might also create certain barriers to digital adoption. Lower digital skills slow down mass adoption of e-commerce solutions and might negatively impact further investments. Lower purchasing power drives consumers' attention towards price-competitive products and offers, which can indeed be easily accessed online, but at the same time are increasingly sourced from cross-border commerce. The growing popularity of AliExpress in the region proves that inexpensive products with attractive delivery options can accelerate online purchases in CEE. However, governments have started to implement legislative measures to promote domestic e-retail and halt the risk of an uneven spread of online traffic towards foreign players. Ordering goods through non-EU-based online platforms is getting more expensive due to new obligatory VAT payments. The most disruptive legislative measures have so far been implemented in the Czech Republic and Russia, but similar procedures have been set up across the region.

Apart from competition coming from cross-border players, domestic e-retailers are facing ongoing challenges of online profitability. Compared to store-based business, even leading online shops struggle to be profitable. The ongoing need for investments in operations, infrastructure, innovation, and technology place a strain on margins across the entire category, and not only in CEE (Tjon Pian Gi and Spielvogel, 2021). Foreign competition from e-commerce giants and consumers' expectation of a frictionless and unexpensive experience makes e-commerce an extremely difficult playing field.

These risks notwithstanding, the e-commerce surge driven by the COVID-19 pandemic allows for a more optimistic approach. The consumer shift to digital purchasing has propelled local companies to invest in innovative digital solutions. The rapidly increasing popularity of e-commerce and m-commerce might be the start of a systemic change in a competition-based digital economy, which, as a result, will further boost innovation, growth of the local talent pool, and the strengthening of CEE's competitive edge.

The digital economy is undoubtedly a major area of future improvement and advancement for CEE. Although societal and economic legacies in the region do not lend themselves to CEE markets rapidly catching up with their Western neighbors, the digital economy, being a nascent sector around the world does allow new players to emerge. Tjon Pian Gi and Spielvogel (2021) outline the following future disruptions in e-commerce landscape:

- highly tailored customer value propositions and higher customer service level
- grocery offerings added by online biggest players and marketplaces, which will improve overall profitability by driving traffic and engagement
- expansion of online product assortments by traditional retailers, increasing private-label penetration.

Players in CEE can leverage the above solutions and deliver consumer-centric strategies that will allow online shopping to maintain the impressive growth curve it currently enjoys. Still, strategies and tactics assumed by businesses will only become sustainable with the concerted digital agenda of respective governments of the region. Iszkowska et al. (2021) outline key measures that should be undertaken by CEE governments and policymakers to facilitate digital transformation:

- support of digitization of the public sector – establishing a structured and convenient system to provide data and support for business-to-business and business-to-government operations; setting standards for digitized consumer journeys and businesses.
- reinforcing competitiveness of CEE businesses through digitization – creation of incubators for promising startups in the region; creation and support of cross-border initiatives between enterprises, by guaranteeing common legal frameworks; facilitating scalability of CEE enterprises, by removing legal and logistical barriers; attracting investors to the region.
- improving availability of the digital talent pool in CEE – conduct and benefit from research aimed at improving digital skills of the entire CEE population; leading CEE-wide initiatives to help attract and integrate digital talents from abroad (Iszkowska et al., 2021, p. 50).

The complexity of CEE's digital transformation lies in consumers' growing digital readiness that is challenged by the macro-economic risks of sloweddown development, insufficient digital education, and low purchasing power. Governments need to strengthen digital innovation ecosystems and support local initiatives that drive innovation, both for business and for consumers (Goyal and Sergi, 2020). Several clusters of scalable innovations are already opening up in the CEE region, such as gaming, software, fintech, and cybersecurity. The success of Allegro and eMag, which achieved their unicorn status as the only ones in the e-commerce sector, prove that scalability of e-commerce is possible and can match and even overtake the strong cross-border players such as Amazon or AliExpress. Innovations and solutions implemented by these companies and multiple smaller players in the region prove that there is strong potential to enhance CEE's e-commerce competitiveness across national and international borders. E-commerce technology can create a more competitive ecosystem, but can also foster cooperation between businesses and companies, by leveraging marketplace models of operations. Multiple e-commerce models, focused on multi-category retailers or mobile-only applications, create new and engaging solutions for consumers but also reinforce further efficiency, effectiveness, and flexibility of the entire e-commerce sector. Governments should encourage growth and stimulate e-commerce entrepreneurship, since it is set up to drive economic growth, especially in the turbulent times caused by the COVID-19 pandemic. The side effect of the pandemic is restriction of outrageous consumerism of pre-pandemic decades, accelerated digitization, and growing importance of green consumption and sustainable lifestyles. The corporate strategists and marketers in CEE should take into account the changing mindset of the contemporary consumers and reformulate their business and marketing strategies to better address the needs of their target audiences during the pandemic and in the post-pandemic era (Maciejewski et al., 2021). E-commerce can be one of the key drivers of sustainable change that will increase digital access and competitiveness of CEE economies.

References

Abrams, K. (2021). *Global E-Commerce Forecast 2021*, New York: eMarketer Insider Intelligence.

Adekola, A. and Sergi, B. S. (2007). *Global Business Management: A Cross-Cultural Perspective*, Aldershot, UK: Ashgate.

Allegro liderem polskiego rynku e-commerce (2020) [Online]. Available at: www.dlahandlu.pl/e-commerce/wiadomosci/allegro-liderem-polskiego-rynku-e-commerce,89671.html (Accessed: 21.06.2021).

Amazon, Allegro, e-commerce w Polsce – jakie są prognozy analityków? (2021) [Online]. Available at: www.dlahandlu.pl/e-commerce/wiadomosci/amazon-allegro-e-commerce-w-polsce-jakie-sa-prognozy-analitykow,98396.html (Accessed: 21.06.2021).

Arnold, S., Chadraba, P., and Springer, P. (2019). Features of Marketing in Central and Eastern Europe. In *Marketing Strategies for Central and Eastern Europe*, New York: Routledge, pp. 4–10.

Aslam, M. M. H. and Azhar, S. M. (2013). Globalisation and Development Challenges for Developing Countries. *International Journal of Economic Policy in Emerging Economies*, 6(2), 158–67.

Banila, N. (2021). Romanian Online Retail Group Books 8.93 bln lei (1.8 bln EUR) in 2020 [Online]. Available at: https://seenews.com/news/romanian-online-retail-group-emag-books-893-bln-lei-18-bln-euro-revenues-in-2020-743118 (Accessed: 30.07.2021).

Beugelsdijk, S., Kostova, K., and Roth, K. (2017). An Overview of Hofstede-inspired Country-Level Culture Research in International Business Since 2006. *Journal of International Business Studies*, 48, 30–47.

Bitzer, J. (2000). An Evolutionary View of Post-socialist Restructuring: From Science and Technology Systems to Innovation Systems. In Ch. Hirschhausen and J. Bitzer, eds., *The Globalization of Industry and Innovation in Eastern Europe. From Post-socialist Restructuring to International Competitiveness*, Cheltenham, UK, Northampton, MA: Edward Elgar, pp. 13–26.

Booth, J. (2020). Visions for 2020: Key Trends Shaping the Digital Marketing Landscape [Online]. Available at: https://blogs.oracle.com/advertising/post/visions-for-2020-key-trends-shaping-the-digital-marketing-landscape (Accessed: 30.06.2021).

Briedis, H., Choi, M., Huang, J., and Kohli, S. (2020). Moving Past Friend or Foe: How to Win with Digital Marketplaces [Online]. Available at: www

.mckinsey.com/industries/retail/our-insights/moving-past-friend-or-foe-how-to-win-with-digital-marketplaces (Accessed: 31.07.2021).

Broadband Coverage in Europe (2019). Luxembourg: European Commission [Online]. Available at: https://digital-strategy.ec.europa.eu/en/library/broad band-coverage-europe-2019 (Accessed: 13.05.2021).

Caccia, W. (2020). E-grocery is Getting Momentum. Is your Brand Seizing Opportunity? [Online]. Available at: www.kantar.com/inspiration/corona virus/egrocery-gains-momentum-is-your-brand-seizing-the-opportunity (Accessed: 01.08.2021).

Cheliński, R. and Szymkowiak, B. (2019). *Cross-Border Commerce – Szansa Czy Zagrożenie?*, Warsaw: Izba Gospodarki Elektronicznej, Poczta Polska.

Chirileasa, A. (2019). Romania's Leading Online E-Retailer eMAG will Enter Third Foreign Market This Year [Online]. Available at: www.romania-insider.com/emag-third-foregin-market-2021-plans (Accessed: 31.07.2021).

Constantin, A. (2019). Four European E-Commerce Leaders, Including eMag, Launch International Marketplace Network [Online]. Available at: https://busi ness-review.eu/news-ro/four-european-ecommerce-leaders-including-emag-launch-international-marketplace-network-205012 (Accessed: 04.07.2021).

Consumer Finance and Retailing in Czech Republic: Euromonitor From Trade Sources & National Statistics (2021) [Online]. Available at: www.portal .euromonitor.com/portal/statisticsevolution/index (Accessed: 14.06.2021).

Consumer Finance and Retailing in Hungary: Euromonitor From Trade Sources & National Statistics (2021) [Online]. Available at: www.portal .euromonitor.com/portal/statisticsevolution/index (Accessed: 14.06.2021).

Consumer Finance and Retailing in Poland: Euromonitor From Trade Sources & National Statistics (2021) [Online]. Available at: www.portal.euromonitor .com/portal/statisticsevolution/index (Accessed: 14.06.2021).

Consumer Finance and Retailing in Romania: Euromonitor From Trade Sources & National Statistics (2021) [Online]. Available at: www.portal .euromonitor.com/portal/statisticsevolution/index (Accessed: 14.06.2021).

Consumer Finance and Retailing in Russia: Euromonitor From Trade Sources & National Statistics (2021) [Online]. Available at: www.portal.euromonitor .com/portal/statisticsevolution/index (Accessed: 14.06.2021).

Consumer Finance and Retailing in Ukraine: Euromonitor From Trade Sources & National Statistics (2021) [Online]. Available at: www.portal.euromonitor .com/portal/statisticsevolution/index (Accessed: 14.06.2021).

Cristea, M. (2021). Romania's E-commerce Grew by a Third in 2020 [Online]. Available at: https://business-review.eu/business/e-commerce/romanias-e-com merce-market-grew-by-a-third-in-2020-216246 (Accessed: 26.06.2021).

Dan, C. (2021a). *E-Commerce in Hungary* [Online]. Available at: www.portal
.euromonitor.com/portal/analysis/tab (Accessed: 24.06.2021).

Dan, C. (2021b). *E-Commerce in Romania* [Online]. Available at: www.portal
.euromonitor.com/portal/analysis/tab (Accessed: 27.06.2021).

Dan, C. (2021c). *Mobile E-Commerce in Hungary* [Online]. Available at: www
.portal.euromonitor.com/portal/analysis/tab (Accessed: 24.06.2021).

Dan, C. (2021d). *Mobile E-Commerce in Romania* [Online]. Available at: www
.portal.euromonitor.com/portal/analysis/tab (Accessed: 27.06.2021).

Eastern and Central Europe eCommerce Explorer: People Payment Trends
(2020) [Online]. Available at: www.rapyd.net/blog/ecommerce-explorer-pay
ment-trends-in-eastern-and-central-europe/ (Accessed: 16.05.2021).

E-Commerce in Bulgaria (2020) [Online]. Available at: https://ecommercenews
.eu/ecommerce-in-europe/ecommerce-in-bulgaria/ (Accessed: 12.04.2021).

E-Commerce in Czech Republic (2021) [Online]. Available at: https://cms
.law/en/int/expert-guides/ecommerce-in-cee/czech-republic (Accessed:
22.06.2021).

Edwards, K. (2021). European E-Commerce Overview: Moldova [Online].
Available at: https://ecommercegermany.com/blog/european-ecommerce-
overview-moldova (Accessed: 25.06.2021).

Escribano, A. and Pena, J. (2021). *Productivity in Emerging Countries.
Methodology and Firm-Level Analysis based on International Enterprise
Business Surveys*, Elements in the Economics of Emerging Markets,
Cambridge: Cambridge University Press.

European E-commerce Report (2019) [Online]. Available at: https://ecom
merce-europe.eu/publications/page/2/ (Accessed: 12.07.2021).

European 2020 Ecommerce Regional Report (2021) [Online]. Available at:
https://retailx.net/product/europe-2020/ (Accessed: 16.05.2021).

Europeans have around EUR 773 less in 2020 due to COVID-19 (2021)
[Online]. Available at: www.gfk.com/press/Europeans-have-around-773-
less-in-2020-due-to-COVID-19 (Accessed: 10.07.2021).

Fleck, J. and Kannengeiser, E. (2020). *Digitalization in Central and Eastern
Europe: Building Regional Cooperation*, Washington, DC: Atlantic
Council.

Galante, N., Garcia-Lopez, E., and Monroe, S. (2013). *The Future of Online
Grocery in Europe*, New York: McKinsey & Company.

Galina, T., Urkmez, T., and Ralf, W. (2018). Cross-cultural Variations in
Consumer Behavior: A Literature Review of International Studies. *South
East European Journal of Economics and Business*, 13, 49–71 [Online].
Available at: http://journal.efsa.unsa.ba/index.php/see/article/view/682/247
(Accessed: 18.07.2021).

Geberen, Á. and Wruuck, P. (2021). *Towards a New Growth Model in CESEE. Convergence and Competitiveness through Smart, Green and Inclusive Investment*, Luxembourg: European Investment Bank.

Gerckens, C., Laizet, F., Läubli, D., and Zgraggen, E. (2021). The Path Forward for European Grocery Retailers [Online]. Available at: www.mckinsey.com/industries/retail/our-insights/the-path-forward-for-european-grocery-retailers (Accessed: 01.08.2021).

Glovo Announces Acquisitions of Delivery Hero in Central and Eastern Europe (2021) [Online]. Available at: https://about.glovoapp.com/en/press/glovo-announces-multiple-acquisitions-of-delivery-hero-in-central-and-eastern-europe/ (Accessed: 01.08.2021).

Goyal, S. L. M. and Sergi, B. S. (2020). *Towards a Theory of 'Smart' Social Infrastructures at the Base of the Pyramid. A Study of India*, Elements in the Economics of Emerging Markets, Cambridge: Cambridge University Press.

Grabiwoda, B. (2018). *E-konsumenci jutra. Pokolenie Z i technologie mobilne*, Warsaw: Wydawnictwo Nieoczywiste.

Grabiwoda, B. and Mróz, B. (2021). Generation Z: The New Mobile Consumers. Empirical Evidence from Poland. *International Journal of Economic Policy in Emerging Economies* (in press).

Harji, R. (2021). Digital Disruption has Taken Hold of Consumer Behaviour (or Vice-Versa). [Online]. Available at: www.itproportal.com/2015/08/29/digital-disruption-taken-hold-consumer-behaviour-or-vice-versa/ (Accessed: 22.05.2021).

Hedley, D. (2007). East is East and West is West. Regional Consumer Attitude Comparisons. [Online]. Available at: https://blog.euromonitor.com/east-is-east-and-west-is-west-regional-consumer-attitude-comparisons-introduction/ (Accessed: 13.07.2021).

Hirschhausen, Ch. and Bitzer, J. (2000). Introduction: Which Industrial and Innovation Policies are Appropriate for Post-socialist Eastern Europe? In Ch. Hirschhausen and J. Bitzer, eds., *The Globalization of Industry and Innovation in Eastern Europe. From Post-socialist Restructuring to International Competitiveness*, Cheltenham, UK, Northampton MA: Edward Elgar, pp. 1–10.

Hirsh, R. (2021). Amazon rozczarował polskim sklepem, więc akcje Allegro drożeją [Online]. Available at: https://businessinsider.com.pl/piec-najciekawszych-wydarzen-w-gospodarce-teraz-raport-03-marca-2021/n76s1k1 (Accessed: 23.06.2021).

Högselius, P. (2005). *The Dynamics of Innovation in Eastern Europe. Lessons from Estonia*, Cheltenham, UK: Edward Elgar.

Hu, H. (2021). *Alibaba Group Holding Ltd. in Retailing (World)*, London: Euromonitor.

Ignatowicz, K., Marciniak, T., Purta, M., et al. (2018). *The Rise of Digital Challengers*, New York: McKinsey & Company.

Iszkowska, J. et al. (2021). *Digital Challengers in the Next Normal*, New York: McKinsey & Company.

Kemp, S. (2021). Digital 2021: Moldova [Online], Available at: https://datareportal.com/reports/digital-2021-moldova (Accessed: 26.06.2021).

Khoruzhyy, I. (2021a). *E-Commerce in Belarus. Country Report* [Online]. Available at: www.portal.euromonitor.com/portal/analysis/tab (Accessed 21.06.2021).

Khoruzhyy, I. (2021b). *E-Commerce in Bulgaria. Country Report* [Online]. Available at: www.portal.euromonitor.com/portal/analysis/tab (Accessed 21. 06.2021).

Khoruzhyy, I. (2021c). *E-Commerce in Ukraine. Country Report* [Online]. Available at: www.portal.euromonitor.com/portal/analysis/tab (Accessed 21.06.2021).

Khoruzhyy, I. (2021d). *Mobile E-Commerce in Belarus. Country Report* [Online]. Available at: www.portal.euromonitor.com/portal/analysis/tab (Accessed 21.06.2021).

Khoruzhyy, I. (2021e). *Mobile E-Commerce in Bulgaria. Country Report* [Online]. Available at: www.portal.euromonitor.com/portal/analysis/tab (Accessed 21.06.2021).

Khoruzhyy, I. (2021f). *Mobile E-Commerce in Ukraine. Country Report* [Online]. Available at: www.portal.euromonitor.com/portal/analysis/tab (Accessed 21.06.2021).

Kohli, S., Timelin, B., Fabius, V., and Moulvard Veranen, S. (2020). *How COVID-19 is Changing Consumer Behavior – Now and Forever*, New York: McKinsey & Company.

Kucia, M., Hajduk, G., Mazurek, G., and Kotula, N. (2021). The Implementation of New Technologies in Customer Value Management – A Sustainable Development Perspective. *Sustainability*, 13(2). [Online]. Available at: www.mdpi.com/2071-1050/13/2/469 (Accessed 24.09.2021).

Labaye, E., Sjatil, P. E., Bogdan, W., et al. (2013). *A New Dawn: Reigniting Growth in Central and Eastern Europe*, New York: McKinsey & Company.

Lamoda Posts 23.5% Sales Growth Year-on-Year, Develops Marketplace Model (2019) [Online]. Available at: www.ewdn.com/2019/06/03/lamoda-sales-records-23-5-sales-growth-year-on-year-develops-marketplace-model/ (Accessed: 31.07.2021).

Lunden, I. (2013). Rocket Internet's "Blitzkrieg". JP Morgan Invests in Russian Fashion Site LaModa [Online]. Available at: https://techcrunch.com/2012/

09/03/jp-morgan-chips-in-for-another-rocket-internet-venture-russian-fash
ion-site-lamoda/ (Accessed: 31.07.2021).

Maciejewski, G., Malinowska, M., Kucharska, B., Kucia, M., and Kolny, B.
(2021). Sustainable Development as a Factor Differentiating Consumer
Behavior: The Case of Poland. *European Research Studies Journal*, 0(3).
[Online]. Available at: https://ideas.repec.org/a/ers/journl/vxxivy2021i3
p934-948.html (Accessed 24.09.2021).

Mander, J., Buckle, Ch., and Hopkins, I. (2020). *Commerce Flagship Report*,
New York: Global Web Index.

Mander, J., Buckle, Ch., and Morris, T. (2020). *Device Flagship Report*,
New York: Global Web Index.

Manyika, J., Lund, S., Bughin, J., et al. (2016). *Digital Globalization. The New
Era of Global Flows*, New York: McKinsey & Company.

Marciniak, T., Novak, J., Pastusiak, B., and Purta, M. (2021). Digital
Challengers in the Next Normal in Central and Eastern Europe [Online].
Available at: www.mckinsey.com/business-functions/mckinsey-digital/our-
insights/digital-challengers-in-the-next-normal-in-central-and-eastern-eur
ope (Accessed: 13.07.2021).

Marrow, A. (2021). AliExpress Russia Looks at Possible IPO, Reports $3
Billion in Transaction Volumes [Online]. Available at: www.reuters.com/
article/us-russia-retail-aliexpress-idUSKBN2BU0RX (Accessed: 01.07
.2021).

Martinez-Ruiz, M. and Moser, K. S. (2019). Studying Consumer Behavior in an
Online Context: The Impact of the Evolution of the World Wide Web for New
Avenues in Research. *Frontiers in Psychology*, 2731(10). [Online]. Available
at: www.frontiersin.org/articles/10.3389/fpsyg.2019.02731/full (Accessed
28.05.2021).

Milasevic, M. (2021a). *E-Commerce in the Czech Republic. Country Report*
[Online]. Available at: www.portal.euromonitor.com/portal/analysis/tab
(Accessed 22.06.2021).

Milasevic, M. (2021b). *E-Commerce in Poland. Country Report* [Online].
Available at: www.portal.euromonitor.com/portal/analysis/tab (Accessed
22.06.2021).

Milasevic, M. (2021c). *E-Commerce in Slovakia. Country Report* [Online].
Available at: www.portal.euromonitor.com/portal/analysis/tab (Accessed
01.07.2021).

Milasevic, M. (2021d). *Mobile E-Commerce in the Czech Republic. Country
Report* [Online]. Available at: www.portal.euromonitor.com/portal/analysis/
tab (Accessed 22.06.2021).

Milasevic, M. (2021e). *Mobile E-Commerce in Poland. Country Report* [Online]. Available at: www.portal.euromonitor.com/portal/analysis/tab (Accessed 22.06.2021).

Milasevic, M. (2021f). *Mobile E-Commerce in Slovakia. Country Report* [Online]. Available at: www.portal.euromonitor.com/portal/analysis/tab (Accessed 22.06.2021).

Mooij, de, M. (2018). *Global Marketing and Advertising. Understanding Cultural Paradoxes*, London: SAGE Publications.

Mróz, B. (2013). *Konsument w globalnej gospodarce. Trzy perspektywy*, Warsaw: Oficyna Wydawnicza Szkoła Główna Handlowa.

Mróz, B. (2021a). Consumers and Businesses Facing the COVID-19 Pandemic: From Shock to "New Normality". In M. Jankowska and M. Pawełczyk, eds., *Fashion Industry Copes with COVID-19. A Legal, Technological and Sociological Reflection*, Katowice: Instytut Prawa Gospodarczego Sp. Z o. o., pp. 35–47.

Mróz, B. (2021b). Consumer Shopping Behaviours on Social Media Platforms: Trends, Challenges, Business Opportunities. In T. Doligalski, M. Goliński and K. Kozłowski, eds., *Disruptive Platforms: Markets, Ecosystems, Monopolists*, Abingdon-New York: Routledge, pp. 113–29.

Namysł, W., Jurkanis, T., Yearwood, K., and Sikora, E. (2019). *Online as the Key Frontline in the European Fashion Market*, New York: McKinsey & Company.

Nolke, A. and Vliegenthart, A. (2009). Enlarging the Varieties of Capitalism: The Emergence of Dependent Market Economies in East Central Europe, Cambridge: Cambridge University Press [Online]. Available at: www .cambridge.org/core/journals/world-politics/article/abs/enlarging-the-var ieties-of-capitalism-the-emergence-of-dependent-market-economies-in-east-central-europe/D4E3D3A7F4ED64CCEDEF71780DAD1547 (Accessed: 12.07.2021).

Novak, J., Filip, A., Valachovicova, I., et al. (2021). *Twelve Million New Online Service Users in CEE* [Online]. Available at: www.mckinsey.com/pl/en/our-insights/digital-challengers-artykul (Accessed: 09.07.2021).

Online Shopping Ever More Popular in 2020 [Online]. Available at: https://ec .europa.eu/eurostat/web/products-eurostat-news/-/ddn-20210217-1 (Accessed: 27.06.2021).

Paunescu, A. (2021). GPeC Romanian E-Commerce 2020 Report: 5.6 Billion EUR Worth of Online Shopping, a +30% YoY Growth [Online]. Available at: www.gpec.ro/blog/en/gpec-romanian-e-commerce-2020-report-5-6-billion-euro-worth-of-online-shopping-a-30-yoy-growth (Accessed: 26.06.2021).

Peterson, M. and Barreto, T. S. (2015). Editor's Introduction: Culture Across Social Sciences. In M. F. Peterson, ed., *Cross-cultural Research*, Vol. 4, pp. 1–4, London: Sage.

Pfirrmann, O. and Walter, G. H. (2002). *Small Firms and Entrepreneurship in Central and Eastern Europe*, Berlin: Springer-Verlag Berlin Heidelberg GmbH.

Poletajevas, B. (2021a). *E-Commerce in Russia. Country Report* [Online]. Available at: www.portal.euromonitor.com/portal/ResultsList/Index (Accessed 28.06.2021).

Poletajevas, B. (2021b). Global Consumer Trends in Eastern Europe [Online]. Available at: https://blog.euromonitor.com/global-consumer-trends-in-eastern-europe/ (Accessed: 18.07.2021).

Poletajevas, B. (2021c). *Mobile Commerce in Russia. Country Report* [Online]. Available at: www.portal.euromonitor.com/portal/ResultsList/Index (Accessed 28.06.2021).

Power, D. (2021). Looking to Get Your Brand Discovered? Why a Niche Online Marketplace Might Be For You [Online]. Available at: www.uschamber.com/co/grow/marketing/how-online-marketplaces-help-new-brands (Accessed: 31.07.2021).

Real GDP Growth Rate (2020) [Online]. Available at: https://ec.europa.eu/eurostat/web/products-datasets/-/tec00115&lang=en (Accessed: 10.04.2021).

Retailing in Belarus: Euromonitor From Trade Sources & National Statistics (2021) [Online]. Available at: www.portal.euromonitor.com/portal/statisticsevolution/index (Accessed: 10.06.2021).

Retailing in Bulgaria: Euromonitor From Trade Sources & National Statistics (2021) [Online]. Available at: www.portal.euromonitor.com/portal/statisticsevolution/index (Accessed: 10.06.2021).

Retailing in Slovakia: Euromonitor From Trade Sources & National Statistics (2021) [Online]. Available at: www.portal.euromonitor.com/portal/statisticsevolution/index (Accessed: 10.06.2021).

Retail mCommerce Sales Growth Worldwide (2021) [Online]. Available at: https://chart-na1.emarketer.com/242923/retail-mcommerce-sales-growth-worldwide-by-region-2021-change (Accessed: 16.05.2021).

Revinova, S. (2019). E-commerce in BRICS: Similarities and Differences. *International Journal of Economic Policy in Emerging Economies*, 12(4), 377–90.

Ribeiro, H. (2020). *Zalando SE Passport – Company Report* [Online]. Available at: www.portal.euromonitor.com/portal/Analysis/Tab# (Accessed: 31.07.2021).

Rosenberg, N. (1983). *Inside the Black Box: Technology and Economics*, Cambridge: Cambridge University Press.

Sass-Staniszewska, P. and Binert, K. (2020). *E-Commerce w Polsce 2020*, Warsaw: Izba Gospodarki Elektronicznej, Gemius.

Selling Online in Belarus (2020) [Online]. Available at: https://merchants .glopal.com/en-us/sell-online/belarus (Accessed: 15.05.2021).

Sergi, B. S., ed. (2019). *Tech, Smart Cities, and Regional Development in Contemporary Russia*, Bingley: Emerald Publishing Limited.

Sergi, B. S., Bagatelas, W. T., and Kubicova J., eds. (2007). *Industries and Markets in Central and Eastern Europe*, Aldershot, UK: Ashgate.

Solomon, M., Bamossy, G., Askegaard, S., and Hogg, M. K. (2010). *Consumer Behaviour: A European Perspective. 4th Edition*, London: Pearson.

Stratten, J. (2020). *Why E-commerce Leader BonPrix's Newest Concept is in Physical Retail* [Online]. Available at: www.insider-trends.com/why-ecommerce-leader-bonprixs-newest-concept-is-in-physical-retail/ (Accessed: 31.07.2021).

Szanyi, M. (2021). Catching-Up Opportunities of East-Central European States in the Context of Technology Cycles. In T. Gerocs, and J. Ricz, eds., *The Post-Crisis Developmental State. Perspectives from the Global Peryphery*, Cham: Palgrave Macmillan, pp. 53–75.

Szanyi, M. and Szabo, G. (2020). Defining the Long-term Development Trends of Countries in East-Central Europe in the Context of Political Cycles. *International Journal of Public Administration* [Online], Available at: www.tandfonline.com/doi/abs/10.1080/01900692.2020.1749850? journalCode=lpad20 (Accessed: 11.07.2021).

Szunomár, A. (2020). *Emerging Market Multinational Enterprises in East Central Europe*, Cham: Palgrave Macmillan.

The e-Commerce Market in Bulgaria (2020) [Online]. Available at: https:// ecommercedb.com/en/markets/bg/all (Accessed: 12.04.2021).

The e-Commerce Market in Russia (2021) [Online]. Available at: https://ecom mercedb.com/en/markets/ru/all (Accessed: 28.06.2021).

Tjon Pian Gi, M. and Spielvogel, J. (2021) [Online]. E-Commerce is Shifting How European Grocery Retailers Seek Profitable Growth [Online]. Available at: www.mckinsey.com/industries/retail/our-insights/e-com merce-is-shifting-how-european-grocery-retailers-seek-profitable-growth (Accessed: 04.07.2021).

Top 100 E-Commerce Retailers in Europe (2020) [Online]. Available at: www.retail-index.com/E-commerceretail.aspx (Accessed: 02.07.2021).

Top Sites Ranking for Lifestyle and Fashion Apparel (2021) [Online]. Available at: www.similarweb.com/top-websites/ukraine/category/lifestyle/fashion-and-apparel/ (Accessed: 04.07.2021).

Tsiotsou, R. H. (2019). Rate my Firm: Cultural Differences in Service Evaluations. *Journal of Services Marketing*, 33(7), 815–36.

Turpin, K., Jędrak, D., Pop, S., and Michnikowska, K. (2021). Exceeding Borders – CEE-17 Retail Report in Times of the Pandemic, *Colliers International* [Online]. Available at: www.colliers.com/en-pl/news/kon dycja-rynkow-handlowych-w-regionie-europy-srodkowo-wschodniej-w-pandemii (Accessed: 16.06.2021).

United Nations Group of Experts on Geographical Names (2021) [Online]. Available at: https://unstats.un.org/unsd/ungegn/divisions/#division-14 (Accessed: 04.03.2021).

Van Rompaey, S. (2021). Online Food Retailer Rohlik Plans European Expansion with Dirsuptive Business Model [Online]. Available at: www .retaildetail.eu/en/news/food/online-food-retailer-rohlik-plans-european-expansion-disruptive-business-model (Accessed: 01.08.2021).

Verscheueren, Ch., Läubli, D., Laizet, F., and D'Auria, G., eds. (2021). *Disruption and Uncertainty. The State of Grocery Retail 2021 in Europe*, New York: McKinsey & Company.

Wamboye, E., Tochkov, K., and Sergi, B. S. (2015). Technology Adoption and Growth in sub-Saharan African Countries. *Comparative Economic Studies*, 57, 136–67.

Yakovlev, A. (2021). On Big Cycles in Development of Global Capitalism. In T. Gerocs and J., Ricz, eds., *The Post-Crisis Developmental State. Perspectives from the Global Peryphery*, Cham: Palgrave Macmillan, pp. 33–53.

Cambridge Elements ≡

Economics of Emerging Markets

Bruno S. Sergi
Harvard University

Editor Bruno S. Sergi is an Instructor at Harvard University, an Associate of the Harvard University Davis Center for Russian and Eurasian Studies and Harvard Ukrainian Research Institute. He is the Academic Series Editor of the Cambridge *Elements in the Economics of Emerging Markets* (Cambridge University Press), a co-editor of the *Lab for Entrepreneurship and Development* book series, and associate editor of *The American Economist*. Concurrently, he teaches International Economics at the University of Messina, Scientific Director of the Lab for Entrepreneurship and Development (LEAD), and a co-founder and Scientific Director of the International Center for Emerging Markets Research at RUDN University in Moscow. He has published over 150 articles in professional journals and twenty-one books as author, co-author, editor, and co-editor.

About the Series

The aim of this Elements series is to deliver state-of-the-art, comprehensive coverage of the knowledge developed to date, including the dynamics and prospects of these economies, focusing on emerging markets' economics, finance, banking, technology advances, trade, demographic challenges, and their economic relations with the rest of the world, as well as the causal factors and limits of economic policy in these markets.

Cambridge Elements ☰

Economics of Emerging Markets

Printed in the United States
by Baker & Taylor Publisher Services